Ancient Architecture

Seton Lloyd / Hans Wolfgang Müller

Ancient Architecture

Electa/Rizzoli NEW YORK

Photographs: Bruno Balestrini
Drawings: Studio Enzo di Grazia
Layout: Arturo Anzani

Library of Congress Cataloging in Publication Data
Müller, Hans Wolfgang.
    Ancient architecture.

    Bibliography: p.
    Includes index.
    1. Architecture, Ancient. I. Lloyd, Seton.
II. Title. NA210.M85 1986 722 85-30006
ISBN 0-8478-0692-8 (U.S.: pbk.)

© Copyright 1980 by
Electa Editrice, Milano

Paperback edition first published
in the United States of America in 1986
by Rizzoli International Publications, Inc.
597 Fifth Avenue, New York, NY 10017

This volume is the redesigned paperback
of the original Italian edition published in 1972
by Electa Editrice, Milan,
and the English edition published in 1974
by Harry N. Abrams, Inc., New York

Printed in Italy

TABLE OF CONTENTS

Architecture of Mesopotamia and the Ancient Near East / Seton Lloyd

THE ORIGINS AND THE PROTODYNASTIC PERIOD

The meaning of the word *architecture* is soberly defined in some dictionaries as "the science of building," though most people would agree that it has in our time acquired a more particularized connotation. It has in fact come to imply the notion of design and the deliberate contrivance thereby of certain aesthetic effects: something other than the mere technology of building construction. This secondary implication should be borne in mind by anyone wishing to study the earliest beginnings of architecture in the ancient world, since he will find himself seeking among primitive peoples the first symptoms of creative ingenuity manifest in the design of buildings. The relevance of this observation will become clear in the pages that follow, since they are concerned with that part of the world which may truly be said to have provided a setting for the birth of architecture. By far the earliest evidence we have of tentative experiments in architectural design is derived from Anatolia and the countries bordering the Syrian Desert; it is the results of archaeological research in this area that we have first to consider.

The incentive to build was initially an outcome of what has been called the Neolithic Revolution: a point of transition in the changing pattern of human behavior, at which the tribal organization of hunters and cave dwellers was discarded in favor of better-coordinated agricultural communities. Much study has in recent years been devoted to this important epoch in human evolution, and certain rather general conclusions have been reached. It is probable that the development began to take place soon after 10,000 B.C., and it is certain that the geographical areas where it originated were the natural homes of wild grains, which provided the raw material of primitive agriculture, and of wild animals destined to become domesticated. The piedmont or semimountainous areas of the Near East answering to these requirements are those in which the remains of very early settled communities have been discovered, and among them evidence has been found of incipient agriculture. Here also we obtain a glimpse of a people in whose memories cave-dwelling must still have been very much alive, and who were now for the first time faced with the need to construct artificial shelters or dwellings.

Needless to say, the forms adopted for the earliest dwellings were dictated by purely practical considerations. Some of the earliest known houses at Jericho in Jordan, dating from the eighth millenium B.C., were circular in plan, with stone foundations and perhaps a clay upper structure. One feels that this may have been an imitation in more permanent materials of tents or other temporary shelters used during a period of nomadism intermediate between cave and village. The materials first used for such permanent dwellings are themselves interesting. Walls of undressed stone, perhaps the oldest and most obvious device, are found only in regions where stone is readily available. Elsewhere, sun-dried clay soon came into use and was universally adopted as the standard building material of the Near East. Tempered with straw, it could initially be built up in slabs in the manner suggested today by the words *pisé* or *adobe*. But at Jericho and elsewhere this clumsy method soon gave way to the use of prefabricated bricks, cast in a rectangular wooden mold and dried in the sun. With this material houses could be built with simple rectangular rooms and roofed with timber.

At a period in the seventh millennium known archaeologically as Prepottery Neolithic B, remarkable advances seem to have been made in brick building. One innovation is again seen at Jericho. Internal wall faces and floors are both neatly rendered in gypsum plaster, which could be stained red and burnished with a smooth stone. The jambs of doorways are carefully rounded to avoid damage to the corners. Even more important in this setting is the plan of a building which its excavator supposes to have been a religious shrine; here for the first time one sees that the design has been considered in relation to the ritual purpose of the building. The entry is through a portico, partly supported on wooden posts; two axially placed doorways lead to an inner sanctuary.

To observe an even more precocious elaboration of architectural ideas in this Neolithic phase of man's development (still in the seventh millenium), one must turn to the site of Catal Huyuk, near Konya in southern Anatolia. Here we are faced not with a village, but with a township covering fifteen or so acres. The houses, built of sun-dried brick, are closely contiguous, almost like the cells of a honeycomb, but each has several rectangular rooms similarly planned, and each is accessible only by a wooden ladder from its flat roof. The roofs are, of course, intercommunicating and provide space for the communal life of the inhabitants. There are many strange features in these buildings. Some of them appear to be religious shrines and are elaborately ornamented with heads or horns of animals, either real or imitated in plaster. The walls are decorated with colored murals, repeatedly repainted after replastering, the designs closely resembling the cave paintings of an earlier cultural phase. As for the ordinary dwelling houses, the main living room has a raised platform to sleep on, and the fireplace is usually located beneath the entry ladder, so that smoke may escape through the open hatch above.

A new element appears in this settlement at Catal Huyuk, namely the necessity for peripheral defense, primarily against wild animals but also probably against the rivalry of other communities. Access to the communal rooftops from outside is again by removable ladders, and the outer house walls are without doors or windows. Returning for a moment to Jericho, one finds there a more familiar and probably more effective provision for defense. Here the excavators exposed the ruins of a huge circular tower built of stone, over twenty-six feet in diameter, and the contingent parts of a defensive wall. By comparison, it is interesting to note that a contemporary or slightly later settlement at Khirokitia on the island of Cyprus seems to have required no form of peripheral defense. Here the houses re-

1. *Jericho, projected plan of Neolithic shrine (from Piggott, 1961).*

2. *Catal Huyuk, portion of town plan, Level VI B (from Mellaart, 1967).*

3. *Catal Huyuk, perspective reconstruction of one section of town, Level VI B (from Mellaart, 1967).*

4. *Catal Huyuk, reconstruction of interior of typical shrine-chamber (from Mellaart, 1967).*

5. *Catal Huyuk, reconstruction of interior of typical house (from Mellaart, 1967).*

6. *Jericho, remains of Neolithic tower.*

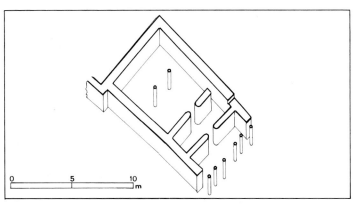

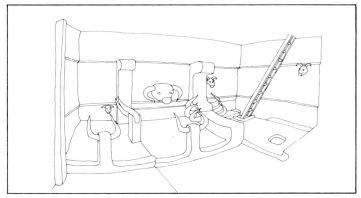

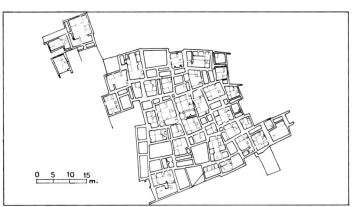

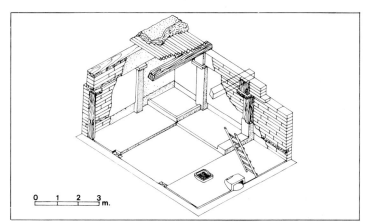

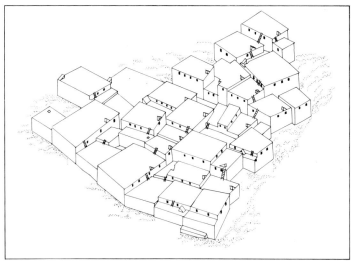

7. *Khriokitia (Cyprus),
reconstruction of Neolithic village
(from Piggott, 1961).*

8. *Hacilar, isometric diagram of
Fortress II A (from Mellaart, 1965).*
9. *Hacilar, isometric diagram of
Neolithic house (from Mellaart,
1965).*

tain an archaic circular form and are roofed with mud-brick domes on a stone substructure. Inside there is an upper floor supported on stone piers and reached by a wooden ladder.

Elsewhere in southern Anatolia, at Hacilar near Burdur, one again sees examples of both these early developments: purposeful planning of buildings and communal defense. A settlement dating from the very end of the Neolithic period shows dwelling houses with a standard plan, in which a prominent domestic hearth between flanking wall-niches is axially placed opposite the entrance doorway. A little later (mid-sixth millennium B.C.), at the beginning of the so-called Chalcolithic period, houses on the periphery of the settlement were knit together to form an outer defense, their lower stories being strongly built with heavy internal buttresses. At this more advanced stage in cultural development it is not surprising to find, at Mersin in Cilicia, a perfectly planned little military fortress. Built of mud brick, again on a stone substructure, the exposed segment has a stone-paved gateway between flanking towers (the first example of a device later to become almost universal) and a stout enclosure wall. Built against the inner face of the wall is a continuous line of identical small buildings providing quarters for the garrison. Each dwelling is provided with two slit-windows in the outside wall, from which the approaches to the mound could be watched, and has a partly roofed yard where piles of sling-stone ammunition could be stored. A more spacious dwelling near the gate was perhaps for the commandant.

Our examples of incipient architectural design, evident so far only in planning, have been drawn from Anatolia and the Levant. In the early centuries of the Chalcolithic Age some of these building conventions had already spread to northern Iraq. The transition, for instance, from nomadic life to that of an agricultural village is well seen at Hassuna, west of the middle Tigris. Here campsites, with the relics of booths built from perishable materials, gave way first to small farmhouses built of pisé clay, then to mud brick. At Arpachiyah, near Nineveh, there seems to have been a reversion to an older pattern of building: circular houses known as tholoi with a rectangular dromos, closely resembling the Mycenaean beehive tombs of three thousand years later. But we must now turn to the alluvial plain of southern Iraq and the marsh country at the head of the Persian Gulf—a region of great importance, since here, in about 5000 B.C., the seeds of Sumerian culture were planted and the first formative elements of monumental architecture came into being.

Geographically, the first arrivals to southern Mesopotamia found a strange setting. Strangely also, the setting has remained unchanged for seven thousand years. Today it provides a background for the lives of the Marsh Arabs, who fish and tend their water buffalo from villages on low islands, in a landscape of interminable reedbeds. Their way of life, too, seems to have remained unchanged since prehistoric times, for they build their houses entirely of reeds, with tall and imposing guest chambers whose

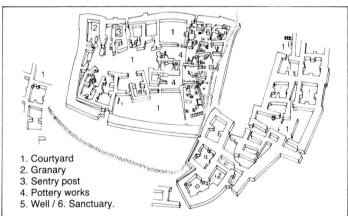

1. Courtyard
2. Granary
3. Sentry post
4. Pottery works
5. Well / 6. Sanctuary.

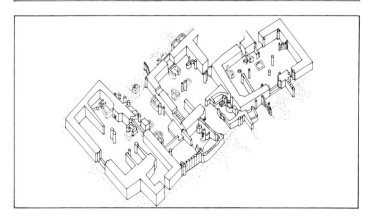

10. *Mersin, isometric diagram of military fortress (from Garstang, 1953).*

11. *Hassuna, isometric reconstruction of farmhouse (from Lloyd, 1961).*
12. *Southern Mesopotamia, modern Arabian reed-built structure.*

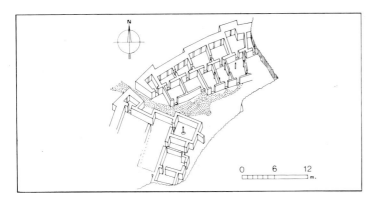

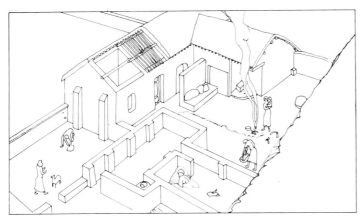

design provides an all-important clue to the forms taken by pre- or proto-Sumerian architecture. These forms are recognizable in the archaic imagery of the Sumerians themselves, particularly in the traditional representation of a temple. Nor can there be any doubt that when the settlers moved inland and more permanent building materials came to be used, the earliest mud-brick temples retained memories of reed construction in their design. The long and fascinating story of Mesopotamian temple architecture, which culminated in the giant ziggurats and palatial temples of Sumer and Babylon, had its beginning in this prehistoric age, and to the end retains suggestions of its reed-built prototypes.

We have then at the site of Eridu, traditionally the oldest holy city of southern Mesopotamia, a sequence of mud-brick temples repeatedly rebuilt during the late fifth and early fourth millennia B.C. It starts with a tiny chapel hardly ten feet square, which has already at least two of the primary elements of such buildings in later times: an altar in a niche facing the doorway, and a small offering table in front of the altar. Later generations elaborated the plan, retaining these elements but elongating the sanctuary and adding lateral chambers on either side. Each building was superimposed on the ruins of its predecessors, so that at an early stage the temple came to stand on a raised platform overlooking the surrounding houses, a development that was later carried to its logical conclusion in the construction of ziggurat towers.

Another feature with which we shall become familiar in observing later temples is the treatment of external facades. Their mud-plastered monotony was relieved by the use of alternating buttresses and recesses, a device whose origin may be traced to the reed buildings of earlier times. This persistent memory of an archaic prototype is equally recognizable in a contemporary group of temples at Tepe Gawra in northern Iraq, an area to which the proto-Sumerian culture had already extended by the end of the fifth millennium B.C. At Tepe Gawra a high elevation constituted from the remains of earlier settlements was crowned by some sort of acropolis, where three very interesting temples were set around an open courtyard. Only the plans of these temples have been recovered, but their somewhat similar arrangement shows facades that are deeply indented, for conventional reasons at which we can only guess. The walls themselves are of surprising fragility. The weight of their roofs must, in fact, have been carried by the more substantial piers with which they were strengthened at regular intervals, thus seeming to resemble the vertical bundles of reeds sustaining the framework of reed dwellings. However this may be, we shall observe from now onward that this type of buttressed facade becomes the most distinctive feature of all religious buildings in Mesopotamia, and is even copied in contemporary Egypt.

The planning of Mesopotamian temples takes an even more definitive form in the so-called Protoliterate period, which dates from the final centuries of the fourth millenium B.C. This was a time when the genius of the

13. *Proto-Sumerian alabaster trough with traditional representation of Sumerian temple. London, British Museum.*

14. *Eridu, plan of temple, Level VII (from Strommenger, 1963).*
15. *Tepe Gawra, perspective reconstruction of group of temples (from Lloyd, 1961).*

Sumerians seems to have reached its zenith, finding expression in some of the cardinal inventions that have contributed to our own civilization. In addition to monumental architecture, the art of sculpture now made its first appearance; the invention of writing foreshadowed the birth of literature and mathematics; and a new talent for social organization brought forth the archetype of the city-state. One Sumerian city whose fame predates the dynastic king-lists of later times was Uruk, the Biblical Erech. Here archaeology has revealed further steps in the evolution of temple architecture. Once again we are presented largely with ground plans, but there are two buildings of which more substantial remains have been found and of which reliable reconstructions can therefore be made. One of these is the so-called White Temple, whose foundations were laid forty feet above street level in the center of the city. The platform on which the temple stood—once more composed from ruins of earlier buildings—had sloping facades of paneled brickwork, and the wall faces of the temple itself showed traces of wooden ornaments between the buttresses. The plan requires some explanation. The long sanctuary and lateral chambers had by now become an accepted convention; the entry for worshippers is through a side room, but there are imposing doorways at either end of the sanctuary itself, one of them displacing the altar from its axial position. Scholars have explained this by attributing to the "high" temple the function of a portal, through which a god could pass on his visits to earth. By contrast, they have postulated a category of "low" temples, in which the presence of the god would be symbolized by a cult statue. For examples of these one must turn to the neighboring Eanna precinct at the same site. Here the plans of a half-dozen temples are presented to us, differing primarily from those hitherto studied only in the fact that the central sanctuary in occasionally cruciform, a pecularity that is also to be seen in a contemporary temple at Tell Brak in northern Iraq.

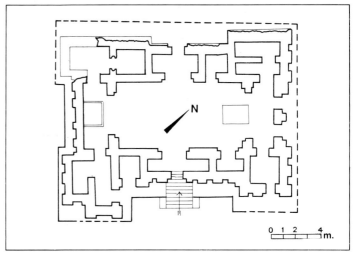

It is also in the Eanna precinct at Uruk that we find our second instance of a better-preserved building. Here two groups of temples are connected by an astonishing portico, supported on colossal circular columns of mud brick and facing a broad open court, whose walls are ornamented with corresponding half columns. A novel and ingenious form of decoration now covers all the interior wall faces of the building. Set in a layer of clay is a mosaic of small terra cotta cones, their heads stained with varying colors to create a sequence of geometrical patterns. Here at last, color and texture are combined to produce a dramatic architectural setting, of the sort that would do credit to a modern decorator. We suspect that this device acquired an even more ambitious form in the last of the temples at Eridu. There, in the external facades, parapets and stringcourses were emphasized by bands of mosaic, sometimes composed of gypsum cones ten inches long whose ends were sheathed in polished copper. At Al 'Uqair in northern Sumer painted murals were substituted for mosaics as internal ornaments in a temple closely resembling the "white" building at Uruk. The

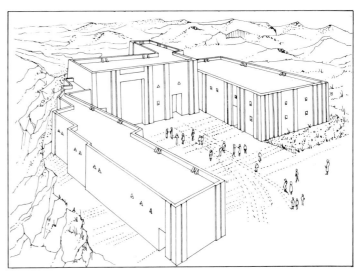

13

16. *Uruk, "White Temple."*

17. *Uruk, perspective reconstruction of "White Temple" (from Piggott, 1961).*

18. *Uruk, integrated plan of ziggurat and "White Temple" (from Strommenger, 1963).*

19. *Uruk, temple plans, Level IV A, Eanna precinct (from Strommenger, 1963).*

20. *Uruk, temple plans, Levels V-VI, Eanna precinct (from Strommenger, 1963).*

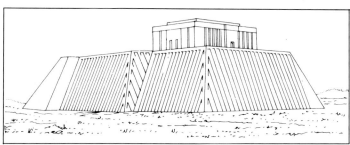

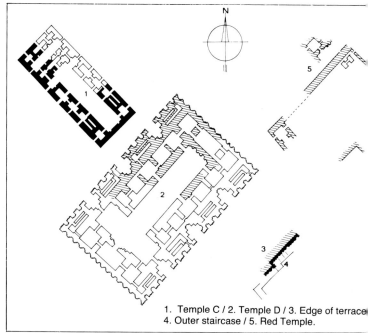

1. Temple C / 2. Temple D / 3. Edge of terrace
4. Outer staircase / 5. Red Temple.

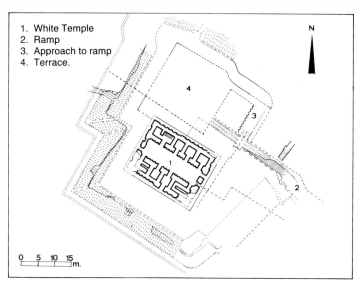

1. White Temple
2. Ramp
3. Approach to ramp
4. Terrace.

0 5 10 15
m.

N

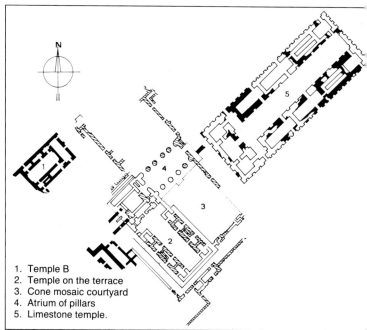

1. Temple B
2. Temple on the terrace
3. Cone mosaic courtyard
4. Atrium of pillars
5. Limestone temple.

subjects used for ornament appear to have been similar to those on the cylinder seals of the period, though the spotted leopards decorating the main altar are an unusual motif.

During the first centuries of the third millennium B.C. a new phase is reached with the founding of the first Sumerian dynasties. Where writing is concerned, primitive pictographs have now been replaced by the cuneiform script, which provides a more convenient vehicle for the Sumerian language. The names of kings and certain political events are now historically recorded. Previously our knowledge of architecture has been largely derived from temples; but dating from the Early Dynastic period there are occasionally palaces to examine and a variety of more modestly planned private houses. The temples, to begin with, show a direct line of development from the Protoliterate buildings we have already discussed. Remnants of only two "high" or platform temples have been discovered, at Khafaje, east of Baghdad, and at Al 'Ubaid, near Ur of the Chaldees. In neither case have remains survived of the temple itself; but the platforms are of some interest, each one having been surrounded at some time by an oval outer wall enclosing a sacred precinct with some subsidiary accommodation. Judging from scanty remains at Ur and Kish, it seems certain that toward the end of this period such platforms had already acquired the stature of ziggurats; but unfortunately at both sites mentioned, later rebuilding has made their examination impracticable. The form also of the temple at their summit can only be surmised on the basis of Protoliterate precedents.

There is, however, one site at which ample evidence was provided, at least regarding the external embellishment of these elevated shrines during the Early Dynastic period. This is at Al 'Ubaid, where a rich collection of facade ornaments had fallen or been removed from the temple when it was intentionally or otherwise destroyed. The platform in this case was faced with kiln-baked bricks and was approached by a projecting stairway with stone treads. It was in the angle between the two that the objects were found, rather carelessly piled together. They included fragments of two freestanding columns, made from palm trunks sheathed in a mosaic of colored stone and mother-of-pearl. Perhaps these originally supported a huge lintel now in the British Museum, a relief panel of hammered copper depicting a mythical lion-headed eagle supported by two stags. There were also copper guardian lions from the doorway, freestanding copper oxen, smaller oxen in relief with projecting heads, and friezes of animals and birds, inlaid in shell or painted limestone against a background of black stone. There has been much speculation regarding the architectural composition of which these objects formed a part, but the tentative reconstructions that have been made lack conviction.

Turning to the "low" or ground-level temples, these are perhaps best represented at sites adjoining the Diyala River and its effluents, such as

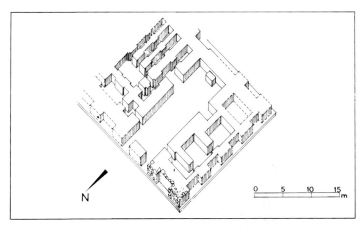

N

0 5 10 15
m

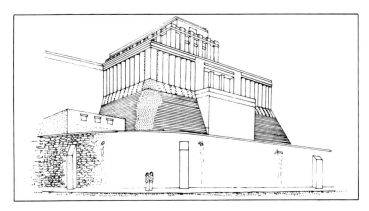

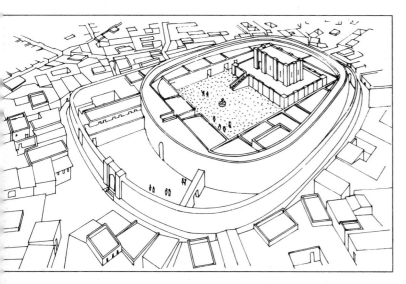

Khafaje. All founded in late Protoliterate times, these have produced a number of temples whose development during the Early Dynastic period can be traced. The old rectangular sanctuary, with its altar, offering table, and entrance on the cross axis, is still the basic element; but in addition to lateral chambers and staircases leading to the flat roof, it now acquires a forecourt surrounded by dependent buildings (Khafaje, Sin Temple), or becomes a symmetrically planned complex with buttressed outer walls, comprising minor sanctuaries in addition to the main shrine (Tell Agrab).

We must now turn to the more modest type of building in which Sumerian families actually lived. Among ruins of the Early Dynastic period, groups of private houses have frequently been found and studied. They are planned—as houses in Near Eastern cities have continued to be planned until quite recently—around a central court from which the surrounding rooms obtained light. Whether the court was occasionally roofed in and light obtained through clerestory windows is at present controversial. Windows were used only internally and then were sometimes protected by a pierced grille of terra cotta. Doorways were covered with wooden lintels or true arches of brickwork. Flat roofs were composed of palm trunks and reeds, covered with earth and plastered with clay. A word should be said about the technique of brick building at this period, since it applies equally to public buildings. Bricks were made in a four-sided wooden mold standing on a flat surface, but the surplus clay, instead of being removed, was rounded off with the hands, thus giving to the brick a loaf shape technically known as *planoconvex*. Such bricks are most ordinarily laid on edge, leaning diagonally against each other in alternate directions so that a herringbone pattern is created on the face of the wall. This habit makes a convenient criterion for identifying buildings of this period.

In the oldest quarter of the Sumerian city at Tell Asmar (Eshnunna) there is a mansion-sized dwelling house built around three separate courts; it can hardly yet be identified as a palace, though it was later rebuilt on a more pretentious scale. Failing here to find the distinctive features of a public building, we should perhaps turn to the complex known as Palace A, at Kish, where two semidetached edifices are enclosed in heavily buttressed outer walls. The larger of the two is again separated from this wall by a protective passage. It is planned around a square courtyard with careful symmetry, but the arrangement of the rooms unfortunately gives no clue to their purpose. The same may be said of the second building, which has two distinctive features: a long rectangular room whose roof was supported on four circular columns of mud brick, and an open loggia, again with circular columns. Many fragments of figured inlay in mother-of-pearl and other materials have been found in these buildings, but their dimensions are hardly great enough to suggest architectural ornament.

So we reach the end of the Early Dynastic period, knowing a great deal more about temples than about buildings dedicated to other purposes. The universal material until now has been mud brick, which is understandable

29. Khafaje, plans of Sin temples
(from Strommenger, 1963).

30. Tell Agrab, plan of Shara
Temple (from Delougaz and Lloyd,
1942).

31. Tell Asmar, plan of Akkadian
palace and contemporary buildings
(from Delougaz, Hill, and Lloyd,
1967).

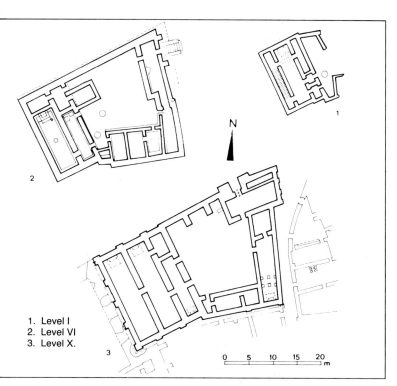

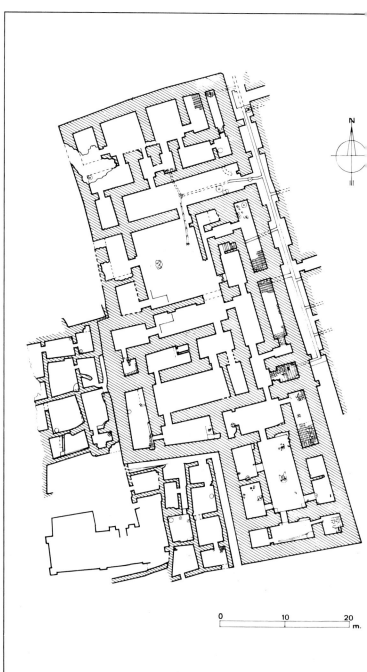

1. Level I
2. Level VI
3. Level X.

0   5   10   15   20
m.

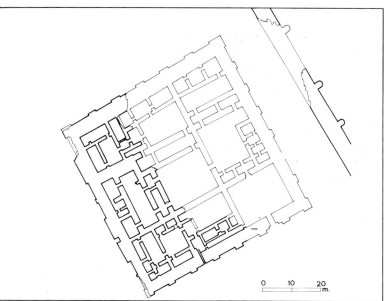

0   10   20
m.

0   10   20
m.

if one remembers the total absence of stone in the alluvial plain of southern Iraq; one does, however, find stone used sparingly at cities on the edge of the plain. At Eridu the whole mound is surrounded by a stone retaining-wall and the temple platform is revetted with stone. At Ur some of the tomb chambers in the Royal Cemetery are built of stone, which can be fashioned into corbeled arches and primitive vaults.

THE DYNASTIC PERIOD

During the twenty-fourth century B.C. the Sumerian city-states were united under a Semitic dynasty founded by King Sargon of Akkad. Little is known about the architecture of this period, since Sargon's capital at Akkad has never been satisfactorily located. It is, however, certain that the Akkadian kings largely rebuilt or repaired the old Sumerian shrines, and two quite interesting secular buildings of this period have actually been excavated. One is the "mansion" house at Tell Asmar, which was now reconstructed on a more impressive scale. Three distinct units have been recognized; their purposes have been provisionally identified by the excavator as, first, the owner's suite with public reception rooms; second, a wing occupied by women; and third, quarters for servants. Each unit was provided with a number of lavatories and bathrooms having an elaborate system of drainage that discharged into a vaulted sewer running along one side of the building. These offices, however, have been differently identified by another authority, who surprisingly prefers to consider the building as a factory or a "guild" headquarters.

A less equivocal building of this period is the palace of Naramsin at Tell Brak in northern Iraq . Square and heavily fortified, it can be identified with some conviction as a military headquarters, with a wide central courtyard and long rectangular chambers grouped around several subsidiary courts. The plan, in its present denuded condition, is otherwise not self-explanatory.

After the fall of the Akkadian empire in about 2230 B.C. there followed a striking revival of Sumerian culture under the Third Dynasty kings of Ur — old cities were again rebuilt and their shrines renovated. Architecturally most characteristic of the times is the layout of the city of Ur at this period. The shape of the walled city corresponded to that of the existing mound, whose sides were now revetted to support a powerful fortification. This great wall, of which little survives today, protected the main residential areas and also two enclosed harbors which gave access to shipping from the Euphrates. The principal public buildings—temples and palaces—were enclosed in an inner fortification, forming a sacred precinct surrounded by a double wall, with storage chambers in the interlying space.

The most conspicuous feature of this group was the great ziggurat standing on its own raised terrace. It was approached through a broad court-

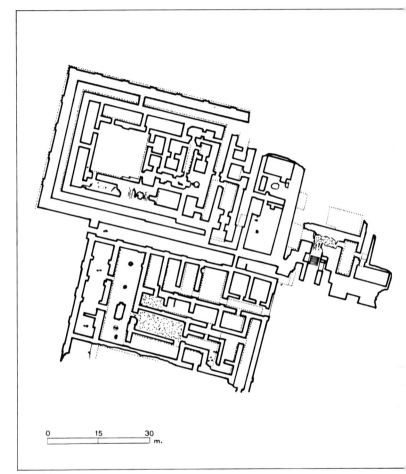

33. *Tell Brak, plan of palace of Naramsin (from Strommenger, 1963).*

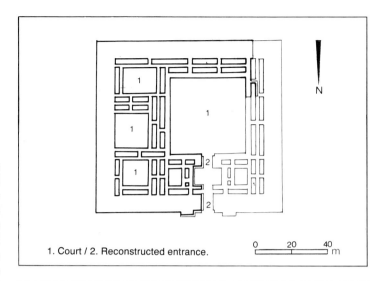

1. Court / 2. Reconstructed entrance.

yard with tower-flanked gateways on all four sides.

This ziggurat is the best preserved and perhaps the best known of the "staged towers" that arose in almost every Sumerian city during this and the subsequent periods. It therefore merits a rather full description. Having evolved, as we have seen, from the raised temples of the Early Dynastic period, its design consists of three successive platforms diminishing in size from the lowest upward and approached by a complicated system of broad stairways. The focal point of the whole structure was of course the temple at its summit; but since this has disappeared, the form it took remains a subject of speculation. For the rest of the building the reconstruction made by Sir Leonard Woolley, after excavation was complete, is based reliably on the most convincing evidence. His description of it reads as follows: "Ur-nammu's building, which also occupied the site of an older and smaller ziggurat, is a rectangle measuring a little more than two hundred feet in length by a hundred and fifty feet in breadth and its original height was about seventy feet. The angles are oriented to the cardinal points of the compass. The whole is a solid mass of brickwork, the core of crude mud bricks, the face covered with a skin, eight feet thick, of burnt bricks set in bitumen... The walls, relieved by broad, shallow buttresses, lean inwards with a pronounced batter, which gives a fine impression of strength, and it is noteworthy that on the ground plan the base of each wall is not a straight line but convex, from which again an idea of strenght results. "Woolley goes on to propose that this deviation was deliberately adopted for aesthetic reasons (though it might be equally attributed to the tumescent effect of so much brickwork). He also notices that the structure was reinforced at intervals with horizontal layers of reeds, sometimes resulting in a form of spontaneous combustion that damaged the fabric. Other refinements are the frequent weep holes intended to release moisture, and the vertical shafts for drainage of rainwater.

The remaining buildings within this central precinct at Ur are architecturally less revealing, since only their plans have been recovered. An understanding of them would require a greater knowledge of religious ritual and hierarchical organization than we now have at our disposal. The two largest are huge square edifices of a type that for want of a better term one might call temple-palaces. A third is clearly a residential palace, and a fourth, asymmetrically planned, has a raised platform accessible from the ziggurat terrace, with a "set of judgment" facing an open courtyard. More interesting structural information is provided by the great mausoleum of the Third Dynasty kings, which lies just outside the limits of the precinct at its eastern corner. Here the burial chambers were sunk beneath ground level, so that their brick vaulting and pointed arches (constructed on a corbeled principle) are comparatively well preserved. They are surmounted by the ruins of funerary chapels whose elaborate ritual installations are again barely explicable.

More easily comprehensible from its plan is a group of buildings at the

Diyala site, Tell Asmar, known as the Gimilsin Temple and Palace of the Governors. Historically, this complex is a bridge between the Third Dynasty of Ur and the subsequent regime at the beginning of the second millennium B.C., when Sumer was once more divided into conflicting principalities. It consists of a substantial temple, dedicated to a deified king of Ur, and a viceroy's palace with its own private chapel for the worship of a local deity. Here we at once observe that the standard planning of temples has adopted a new formula, which was destined to persist throughout the remaining history of Mesopotamian architecture. The whole building is now arranged on a single main axis, which passes through the center of the building, from the tower-flanked gateway across the central court to the sanctuary itself, terminating in the high altar with its cult statue. As for the adjoining palace, its interest is concentrated in the reception suite, a combination of features subsequently recognizable in all Babylonian palaces. A throne room is entered by a central doorway in one of its long sides, while smaller doors lead to a great hall or council chamber with adjacent retiring rooms and a staircase leading to the flat roof.

After the fall of Ur this group was repeatedly rebuilt by the independent governors of Eshnunna; but the dedication of the main temple had lost its relevance and its ruins were soon incorporated in the palace. In a well-known architectural reconstruction of its original form, some features of the upper structure are necessarily hypothetical. Little has till now been said on this subject, simply because so little is in fact known, but its discussion will be resumed in connection with buildings of later periods for which evidence is more plentiful. For the present, only bare facts can be mentioned. Walls, for instance, are built of large, prismatic mud bricks, faced with mud plaster within and without. Facades are still decorated with buttresses and towers, with multiple recessing in the form of vertical grooves. Kiln-baked bricks are reserved for pavements and, in conjunction with bitumen, for wall facing in settings where water is used.

The two earliest centuries of the second millennium B.C., which preceded the unification of Mesopotamia under Hammurabi of Babylon, have provided us with two unique examples of contemporary architecture, one a temple and the other a palace. The temple is a huge, complex building associated with the worship of a goddess called Ishtar-Kititum, at the Diyala site called Ischali. It is composed of three units, each a temple in its own right with its appropriate courtyards and dependencies, all skillfully united in a coherent and magnificent architectural composition. One-third of the complex stands at a higher level than the rest and contains the sanctuary of Ishtar herself, with a spacious treasury behind it. It can be approached either axially from the street outside or less directly from the enormous main courtyard by a flight of steps. One of the two subsidiary shrines can be entered from outside in the same way, but the other has reverted to an older tradition, with its approach at right angles to the true axis. All the main gateways are guarded by twin towers with grooved or-

namentation. For the rest, the building requires little further comment, since its appearance is represented faithfully in the fine wash drawing by the late Harold Hill illustrated here.

The second building we have noted is in northern Iraq, on the middle Euphrates—the palace of Zimrilim, an independent ruler of the state called Mari. This building has been rather floridly described as "a jewel of archaic oriental architecture." If one considers its size—it has about three hundred rooms and covers an area of seventeen acres, rather more than the contemporary city of Troy—as well as its indications of interior decoration, this description becomes less fanciful. As will be found in comparable buildings of later times, the life of the building seems to be concentrated around two major courtyards, one to which the public had access and another to which only the royal family and its immediate dependents were admitted. Facing the outer courtyard and reached by steps was an audience chamber with a throne emplacement, which must have brought the ruler into direct contact with his people. The kings of Mari were of Semitic origin, and it is tempting to see in this chamber, with its open-ended planning, a prototype of the vaulted *iwan*, which served the same purpose in Oriental palaces of the Moslem era. Turning to the inner courtyard, one finds two huge chambers, entered successively through a central doorway in the south wall, and one is first inclined to equate these with the throne room and great hall of the Babylonian reception suite, especially as the first chamber has a throne emplacement opposite the entrance. One finds, however, that there is a suggestion of religious ritual about this suite, for the larger chamber has at one end a raised sanctuary, approached by a flight of steps, toward which a throne at the other end faces.

A carefully segregated unit in the northwest corner of the building is easily recognizable as the ruler's own residential suite. Protected on the outside by double walls and a heavy filling of rubble, it has such amenities as bathrooms and mural ornament in the principal rooms. A smaller room, conveniently placed between this apartment and the inner courtyard, contained the now famous palace archive of cuneiform tablets, through which much has been learned about the history of the period. Also closely adjoining the royal suite is a school for scribes or a clerical department. In the surrounding labyrinth of chambers some, such as the treasury, storerooms, and domestic offices, can be positively identified; others remain anonymous.

Striking features of the palace's interior decoration are the figured mural paintings that once adorned the walls, notably in the audience chamber and on the south side of the inner courtyard, which was protected by a canopy roof supported on posts. The paintings themselves, in which the excavators detected traces of true fresco technique, show elaborate ritual scenes, such as a sacrificial procession or an investiture, and are of great archaeological interest.

Much impressive sculpture was also found, but the fragments were scat-

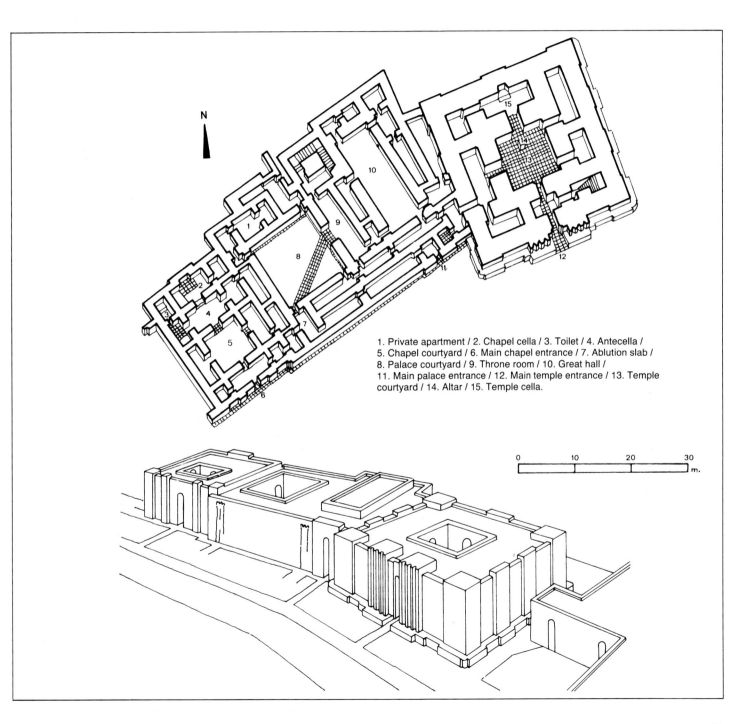

37. Tell Asmar, plan and reconstruction of temple of Gimilsin and palace of the Governors (from Frankfort and Lloyd, 1940).

1. Private apartment / 2. Chapel cella / 3. Toilet / 4. Antecella / 5. Chapel courtyard / 6. Main chapel entrance / 7. Ablution slab / 8. Palace courtyard / 9. Throne room / 10. Great hall / 11. Main palace entrance / 12. Main temple entrance / 13. Temple courtyard / 14. Altar / 15. Temple cella.

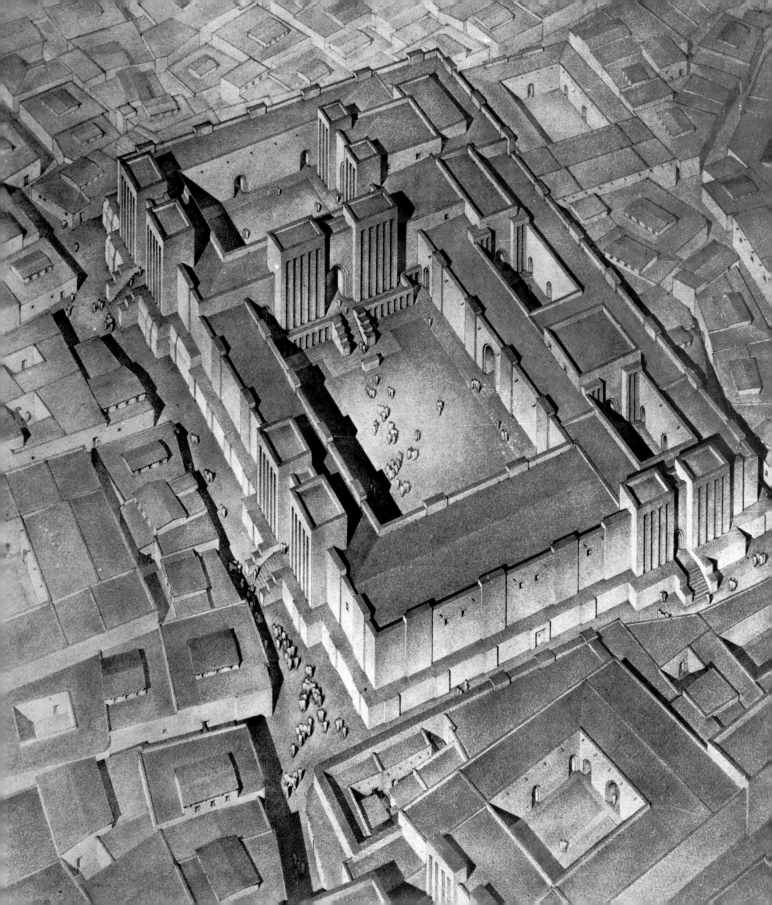

38. Ischali, perspective
reconstruction of temple of
Ishtar-Kititum (from Harold
D. Hill).

39. Mari, plan of palace of
Zimrilim (from Portoghesi,
1968-69).
40. Mari, mural paintings from
palace of Zimrilim. Paris, Louvre.

tered, and its place in the architectural decor remains uncertain.

At one point in the history of Mari the city was annexed and the palace occupied by Assyria, a newly prominent state with its capital at Assur on the middle Tigris. During the remaining centuries of the second millennium B.C. Assyria played a leading role in the history of Mesopotamia. But before studying Assyrian architecture we should take one more look at contemporary events in Babylonia. In about 1600 B.C. southern Mesopotamia fell under the dominion of the Kassites, an intrusive Indo-European people from beyond the Zagros Mountains, and for almost four centuries Babylonia was ruled by a line of Kassite kings. The replacement of Hammurabi's dynasty by an alien aristocracy had surprisingly little effect on the basically Sumerian culture of the country, since its new rulers simply adopted the political and religious conventions they found there, repairing and often rebuilding the age-old monuments of the Sumerian cities. They did, however, found a new capital city at Dur Kurigalzu (Aqar Quf), whose ruins have been partially excavated. The denuded core of its huge ziggurat—heavy mud brick reinforced with matting and three-inch cables of twisted reeds—makes a striking landmark in the desert west of modern Baghdad. The temples and palaces surrounding it show some novel architectural features. One innovation, to be seen in the courtyard of a royal palace, is the use of mural painting to form an ornamental dado at the base of external walls, thus anticipating the relief sculptures used for the same purpose in later Assyrian buildings. A Kassite temple at Uruk again creates a precedent in facade ornament. This takes the form of clay figures that were modeled in rilief, cut into bricks before drying, and reconstitued after backing in a kiln. This technique, as we shall see, was further developed in Late Assyrian and Neo-Babylonian times.

To return now to the oldest Assyrian capital at Assur, we find a city strategically placed and heavily fortified. It stands on a prominent outcrop of limestone overlooking the Tigris, whose waters protect it on two sides. Its defenses are completed by a powerful city wall, rebuilt at least once and extended to give greater living space. Its temples and palaces, which occupy the elevated northern quarter, have a complicated architectural history testifying in some cases to almost a thousand years of continual occupation. There are, to begin with, no less than three ziggurats, the largest dedicated to the city god, Assur. Two others, with a temple between them, are associated with the gods Anu and Adad. A fourth, outside the city and again having its own "low" temple annexed to it, was dedicated to Assur by Tukulti-Ninurta I in the thirteenth century B.C. In all these towers the great triple stairway that we have seen at Ur is missing, and there is still some doubt as to how their summits were reached. Perhaps the approach was from the flat roofs of adjoining buildings.

A good example of Early Assyrian temple planning is to be seen in the Ishtar temple at Assur. Its first foundation was in Sumerian times and consisted of a single rectangular sanctuary, similar to those we have noted

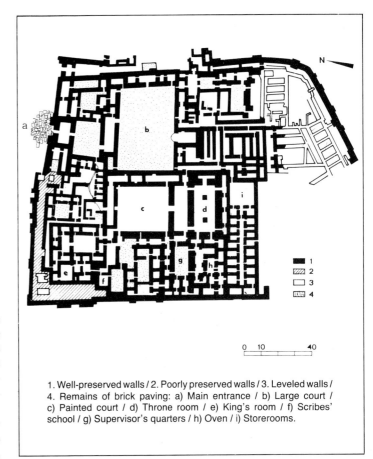

1. Well-preserved walls / 2. Poorly preserved walls / 3. Leveled walls / 4. Remains of brick paving: a) Main entrance / b) Large court / c) Painted court / d) Throne room / e) King's room / f) Scribes' school / g) Supervisor's quarters / h) Oven / i) Storerooms.

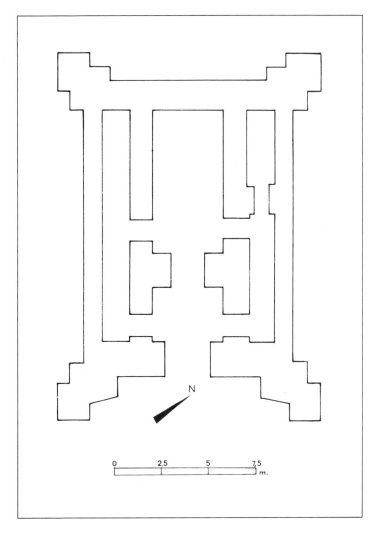

earlier in Sumer itself. By the thirteenth century B.C. it had acquired side chambers and a small subsidiary shrine at one corner, but both sanctuaries were still entered on the cross axis. A distinctively Assyrian feature, however, was the withdrawal of the main altar to an elevated alcove approached by a broad flight of steps, thus separating the worshipers from the shrine itself.

Having now reached the final centuries of the second millenium B.C., we are at last able to know something more about the facade treatment and general outward appearance of temples and palaces. We know, for instance, that the towers flanking entrance gateways, like those projecting at intervals from the city walls, rose to a greater height than the walls themselves, and were decorated with small windows, either real or false. We also know from representations on cylinder seals that both these towers and the walls themselves terminated in crenellated parapets, sometimes projecting slightly beyond the wall face. As for the mud-brick facades, the custom of creating vertical emphasis by means of recessed grooves or corrugated reeding had recently been elaborated to a surprising degree by the introduction of engaged or even freestanding columns, spirally carved or modeled to represent palm trunks. Examples of such ornament have been found in a Kassite setting at Ur, and again in a Middle Assyrian temple far to the north at Tell Rimah. Recent excavations at this last site have also removed once and for all any previous doubts about the proficiency of Mesopotamian architects at mud-brick vaulting. In a ziggurat temple at Tell Rimah surviving fragments have been found of elaborate vaulting, already based on a true-arch principle. Little more remains to be said about the decoration of internal wall faces. Orthostatic slabs of stone, such as were used in the Late Assyrian palaces, had not yet been adopted; but a similar feature, composed of painted and glazed terra cotta panels, has been found in the thirteenth-century palace at Kar Tukulti-Ninurta, near Assur. In a position higher on the wall, mural paintings were still used, for example in the Hurrian palace at Nuzi, near Kirkuk, where the ornamental motifs already suggest contacts with Egypt and Mycenae or Crete.

Anatolia and the Hittite Domination
In our discussion of architecture in the Near East prior to the end of the second millennium B.C., our range of vision has so far been limited largely to the frontiers of Mesopotamia. If our attention is now turned to Anatolia—the great land bridge of Asia Minor that connects Mesopotamia with eastern Europe—we shall find ourselves faced with a notable time lag in the development of monumental building. Here, dating from the Early Bronze Age—which accounts for the greater part of the third millennium B.C.—few buildings have survived that have any pretension to be considered as architecture. One type in particular seems at this time to be conspicuously absent, namely, the temple. No building of this period has

hitherto been positively identified as such; religious shrines amount to no more than semicomprehensible assemblages of ritual installations in buildings of a crude simplicity, which has led some scholars to identify them as mere private houses. Where secular buildings and fortifications are concerned, we are on firmer ground, and in this respect the excavations of the city of Troy have exposed some of the best examples.

During its life span of almost two and one-half thousand years, from early in the third millennium B.C. to the time of Alexander the Great, the famous fortress at Troy was rebuilt repeatedly and often extended or replanned. Of the buildings thought to be contemporary with the Trojan War (Level VII A) almost nothing remains, owing to the decapitation of the mound in later times; but below this level the fortifications at least are better preserved, and in one stratum (Level II G), dating from the Early Bronze Age, the plan of almost the whole fortress has been more or less convincingly reconstructed. The enclosure wall has a substructure of dressed stone, slightly battered or inclined to give it greater strength, and the single gate in use at this time is protected by a transverse tower structure with a narrow ascending ramp. From the layout of buildings within the walls the first inference to be made is that this cannot be described justifiably as a city. Excavations have shown that in Homeric times its area was slightly extended; but with a diameter of less than 150 yards the word *fortress* still seems more applicable. Apart from groups of rather carelessly planned private dwellings, and a "palace" on the western side—beneath which Schliemann unearthed the caches of gold jewelry that he called Priam's Treasure—the most conspicuous feature of the plan is the great building in the center with its rectangular hall, open portico, and enormous central hearth. This barnlike structure, with a breadth of almost twenty-five feet from wall to wall, is of special interest, as it represents an early example of the hall-and-porch plan that is later known to the Greeks as a *megaron* and that eventually reappears as the central element of the Classical temple. The origin of the megaron is buried in the prehistory of western Anatolia, where it appears from time to time as the basic plan for the Bronze Age dwelling house, until it is transmitted, probably by the Phrygians, to Greece. Its outstanding characteristics are the huge circular hearth, the "sleeping platforms" in the portico, and the occasional facings of stone or timber (parastades) on the outer ends of the projecting wings. One variant, incorporated as the central element of more elaborately planned buildings, is seen fully developed in the megaron halls of palaces at Mycenae and Tiryns, but its counterpart is already found a thousand years earlier in an Early Bronze Age building excavated at Kultepe (the ancient Kanesh) in Cappadocia.

In Anatolia during the latter half of the second millennium B.C. architecture once more came into its own. A number of powerful states now contested the supremacy of the peninsula. Of these the Hittite kingdom is best known for the architectural monuments it has bequeathed to us, some sur-

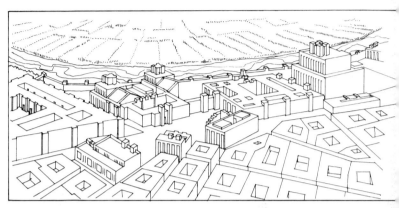

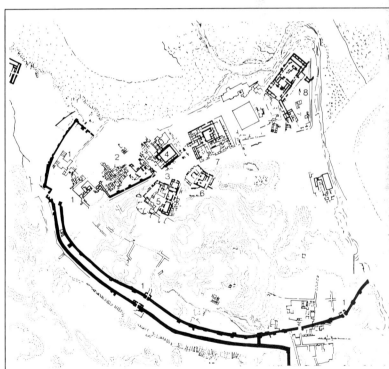

1. Portal / 2. New Palace / 3. Temple plaza / 4. Temple of Anu and Adad / 5. Ishar / 6. Temple of Sin and Shamash / 7. Old Palace / 8. Temple of Assur.

46. *Assur, plans (from Frankfort, 1954; and Strommenger, 1963).*
A. Ziggurat of Tukulti-Ninurta I /
B. Temple of Anu and Adad /
C. Temple of Ishtar

47. *Assur, reconstruction of mural paintings, palace of Kar Tukulti-Ninurta I.*

48. *Nuzi, fragment of mural paintings, palace of Hurrian.*

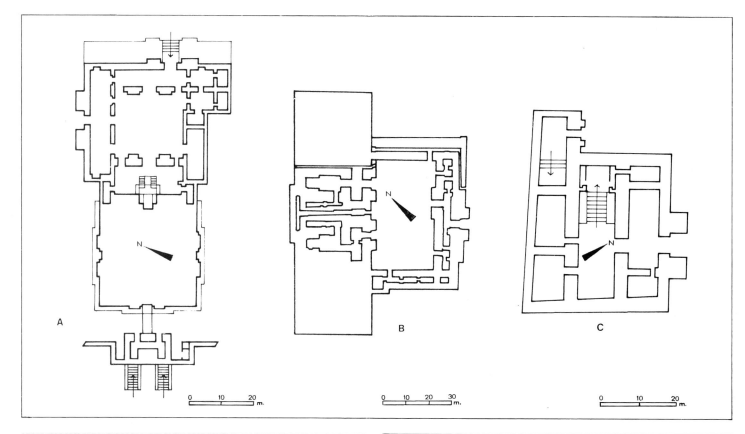

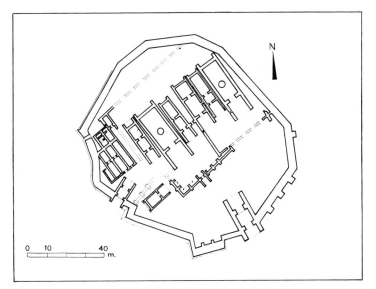

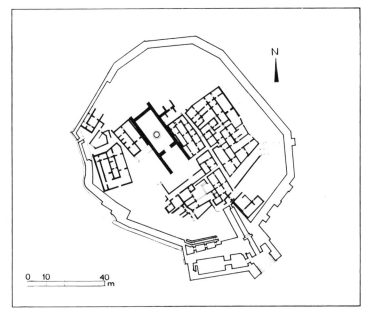

49,50. Troy, plans of city, Levels I and II (from Anatolian Studies, 1959).

51. Troy, reconstruction of surviving walls, Level VI (from Naumann, 1955).

viving above ground and others recovered by laborious excavation. Its territory, first confined to a province within the curve of the Halys River, was greatly extended by conquest during the fourteenth and thirteenth centuries B.C., when Hittite armies fought on equal terms with those of Egypt and Mesopotamia. During this time the Hittite capital was at Hattusas, now known to the Turks as Bogazkoy, where a four-mile circuit of powerfully built city walls dating from the fourteenth century B.C. can still be seen. The very size of the city testifies to the imperial greatness of the Hittite people. Strategically placed astride a rocky gorge, an inner enclosure—representing the earliest foundation—rises up toward the high citadel rock, Buyukkale. The greatly extended outer city was protected by a line of fortifications whose complexity anticipated the engineering accomplishments of much later times. The double walls, with their defensive towers and substructure of cyclopean masonry, stand on a stone-faced rampart of earth, itself protected by an outer apron wall of stone. Some of the many gates, with arched openings, are flanked by sculptured figures of lions or sphinxes, anticipating by five centuries the guardian sculptures of Late Assyrian buildings. Within the city, stonebuilt temples are once more in order; of the largest example, called Temple I, a plan is here reproduced. It will be observed that the main sanctuary, isolated in a separate wing on the northeast side, and the great courtyard, with its pillared colonnade and small freestanding shrine in one corner, have nothing in common with the conventions of contemporary Mesopotamian architecture. The plan of another temple has also been recovered, near the entrance to the famous sculptured caves at Yasilikaya, outside the town. It is approached through an interesting freestanding propylon.

All these buildings, including the city walls themselves, had upper structures of sun-dried brick, of which few traces remain. In order to study this form of construction we must therefore turn to the houses of the rich Assyrian merchants at Kultepe (Kanesh I b) or to the Arzawan palace at Beycesultan. Both provide examples of a building principle already universally adopted throughout Anatolia at that time, which by modern analogy should be described as half-timbered construction. Above their stone foundations the walls consist of a stout timber framework with panels of brick filling in between. In the Beycesultan palace the stone substructure itself was founded upon transverse logs of wood, and the quantity of timber incorporated in the galleried upper story may be judged from the ample evidence of its destruction by fire.

It has been suggested that this long-surviving tradition of timber-frame construction—used to this day throughout Anatolia and in parts of the Levant—was originally devised and adopted as a precaution against earthquakes, affording as it does a certain elasticity to mud-brick structures. Rarely, if ever, to be seen in Mesopotamia, where earthquakes seldom occur, it extends into northern Syria and can be studied in two historic buildings of the second millennium excavated at Tell Atchana in the Plain

of Antioch. Both are the residences of local rulers, one called Yarimlim, who was a contemporary of Hammurabi in the eighteenth century B.C., and the other Niqmepa, who ruled some two and one-half centuries later. Neither building is very ambitiously planned, but both incorporate two architectural innovations, from now on increasingly characteristic of Syrian building. One is the basalt orthostats used in the Yarimlim palace as revetment for the lower part of the walls which creates an important precedent. The other, seen at the approach to the main reception room in this building and again at the entry to Niqmepa's residence, is a screen of circular wooden columns on basalt bases, forming a portico of the sort which, as we shall see presently, will become the central feature of the so-called *bît-hilani* palaces of Iron Age Syria. One other feature of the eighteenth-century palace should also be noted. The most richly equipped residential rooms, those located southeast of the main courtyard, occupied an upper story, a so-called piano nobile, an arrangement also to be seen at Beycesultan in western Anatolia and, too, by the palace at Knossos.

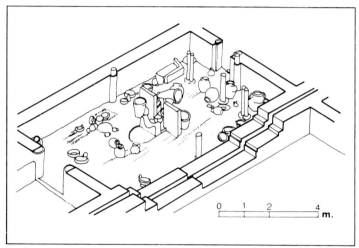

The Neo-Assyrian Period

We must now return to Mesopotamia, and observe the prodigies of building activity achieved by the Assyrian kings during the earlier part of the first millennium B.C. This period, during which Assyria attained the status of a great imperial power, may be said to date from the reign of Assurnasirpal II (883-859 B.C.), who transferred his headquarters from ancient Assur to a newly built capital city at Nimrud (Calah), twenty-two miles south of modern Mosul. Later kings ruled from Nineveh, which lies on the left bank of the Tigris opposite Mosul itself, while Sargon II, like Assurbanipal, built his own capital at Khorsabad in the hilly country to the northeast. All three of these great cities have been excavated repeatedly during the past century, and successive generations of archaeologists have recorded their architecture. If we examine their planning and layout, they will be found to have much in common. In each case the site had been occupied already by a small town or village settlement, whose remains had created a useful elevation. The top of the existing mound could therefore be leveled and extended to create a raised platform on which the principal public buildings of the new city were placed. From either side of the platform, lines of protective walls extended to enclose a residential area adequate to the requirements of a capital city. At Nimrud the mound was skirted on two sides by the waters of the Tigris and of a major irrigation canal, so that the platform needed to be revetted with a stone quay wall. At the summit the palaces and temples built by successive kings were laid out with little coherent planning. The remains of a small ziggurat occupy one corner. The lower city also seems to have been irregularly planned, but its periphery measured almost five miles. Nineveh was even larger, covering an area of two and one-half square miles, and it had two palace platforms, Kuyunjik and Nebi Yunus, rather close together. A moat surrounded the

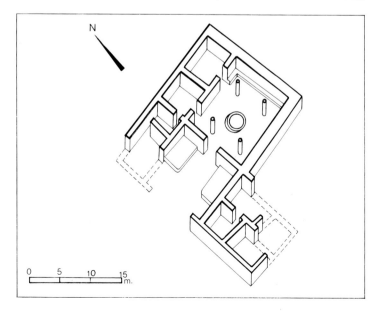

55. Bogazkoy, plan of citadel of Buyukkale (from Akurgal, 1962).

56. Bogazkoy, reconstruction and section of walls and gate (from Akurgal, 1962).

57. Bogazkoy, Lion Gate.

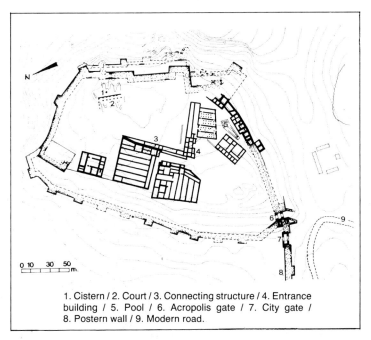

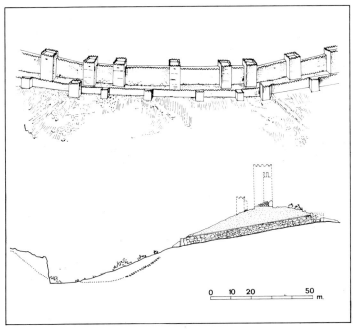

1. Cistern / 2. Court / 3. Connecting structure / 4. Entrance building / 5. Pool / 6. Acropolis gate / 7. City gate / 8. Postern wall / 9. Modern road.

IV. Gordion, city wall.

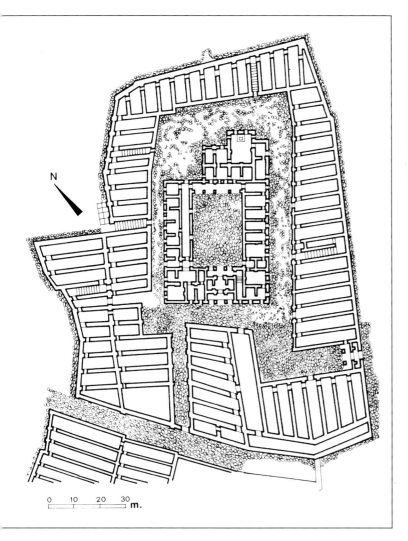

60. Bogazkoy, plan of Temple I and surrounding storerooms (from Akurgal, 1962).

61. Bogazkoy, relief of war god from King's Gate. Ankara, Museum.

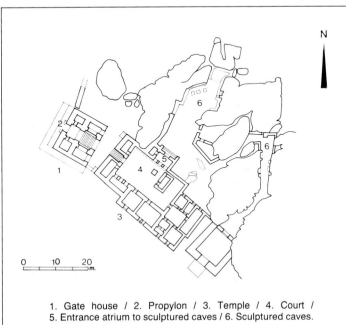

1. Gate house / 2. Propylon / 3. Temple / 4. Court /
5. Entrance atrium to sculptured caves / 6. Sculptured caves.

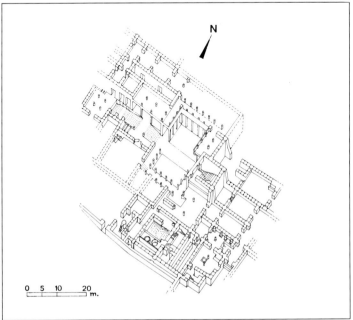

66. *Tell Atchana, plan of palace
of Yarimlin (from Frankfort, 1954).*
67. *Tell Atchana, plan of palace
of Niqmepa (from Frankfort, 1954).*

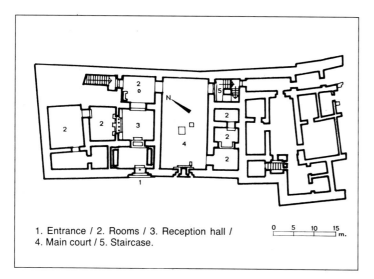

1. Entrance / 2. Rooms / 3. Reception hall /
4. Main court / 5. Staircase.

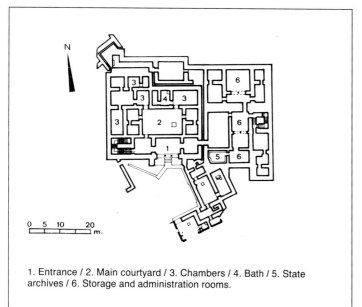

1. Entrance / 2. Main courtyard / 3. Chambers / 4. Bath / 5. State
archives / 6. Storage and administration rooms.

walls not protected by the Tigris, and there were many towered gateways, some decorated with sculpture.

Sargon II's palace at Khorsabad is of particular interest because it was built on an open site, previously unoccupied except for the usual small mound representing the remains of an earlier village. From this a palace platform was created astride the city walls, which themselves enclose an area of one square mile. Built of solid mud brick more than twenty feet thick, the walls have towered facades and seven monumental gateways. At the base of the palace platform inside the city there is a walled citadel containing several minor palaces and one important temple, dedicated to the god Nabu. In a remote position near the southeast corner of the city there is a second raised palace, known as Palace F, of the type called *ekal mashati*, which was used for assembling military equipment and storing the spoils of war. This must be compared with "Fort Shalmaneser" at Nimrud, which occupies a site equally remote from the main citadel. These primary public buildings at Khorsabad have been well excavated and deserve more detailed study; some initial comment on their architecture applies equally to their counterparts at Nimrud and Nineveh.

Our discussions of Mesopotamian architecture till now have been primarily concerned with the design of temples. In this Late Assyrian period greater emphasis came to be placed upon royal palaces, to which the temples appear subsidiary. Owing to their state of preservation and the circumstances of their excavation, far more is known about the planning and contents of these palace buildings than about their superstructure and architectural appearance. In this sense a major compensation has been the sculptures with which the lower parts of their walls were usually adorned. The interior wall faces of the principal chambers were decorated with sculptured reliefs up to a maximum height of about nine feet, while the external doorways were flanked by guardian figures of human-headed bulls or lions sculptured in stone. Built into the reveals and appearing to support the semicircular archways above, these are usually double-aspect figures with five legs, to be viewed either from in front or from the sides. A great deal has been written about Assyrian sculpture; as a document of Assyrian life the reliefs have proved an invaluable supplement to the written texts. Less is generally known about the technology of their installation. The bases of the largest portal figures measured almost twenty square feet and must have weighed approximately twenty-five tons. Roughly cut to the required shape, the stone was transported from the quarry, partly by rivercraft, and the sculpture completed in situ. The orthostat reliefs also had to be carved in situ—since the pictures on them overran from one slab to the next—and this was done before the mud-brick upper structure of the walls was completed. The touches of color enlivening the sculptures may have been applied later.

The study of planning has been hampered by our comparative ignorance of secular ritual and domestic behavior in Assyrian times. Some aspects,

68. Khorsabad, plan of city (from Strommenger, 1963).

69. Khorsabad, plan of Royal Palace of Sargon II, including temple complex (right); plan of temples in Royal Palace (left) (from Strommenger, 1963).

70. Nimrud, plan of palace platform (from Mallowan, 1966).

71. Nimrud, plan of Fort Shalmaneser (from Mallowan, 1966).

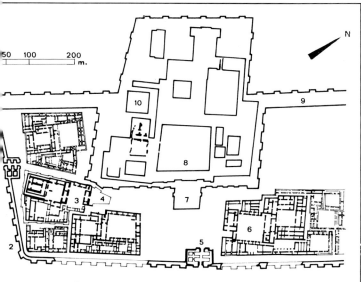

1. Portal A / 2. Citadel walls / 3. Temple of Nabu / 4. Ramp / 5. Portal B / 6. Palace of Sinahasur / 7. Ramp / 8. Palace of Sargon / 9. City walls / 10. Ziggurat.

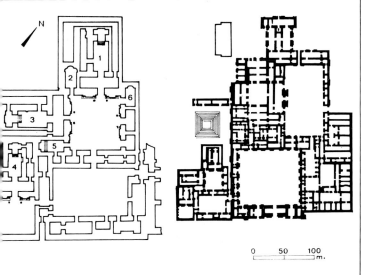

1. Temple of moon god Sin / 2. Temple of weather god Adad / 3. Temple of sun god Shamash / 4. Temple of Ningal / 5. Temple of god of war and the hunt, Ninurta / 6. Temple of god of wisdom and the ocean, Ea.

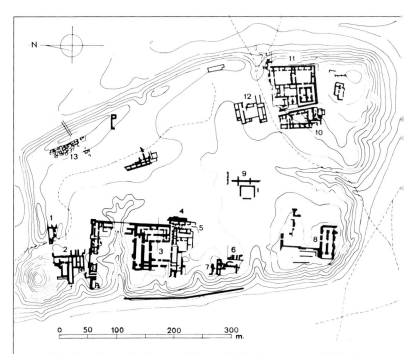

1. Temple of Ishtar / 2. Temple of Ninurta / 3. Northwest palace / 4. Serving room well / 6. Palace of Adad-Nirari III / 7. Upper rooms / 8. Southwest palace / 9. Central palace / 10. Burned palace / 11. Temple of Nabu / 12. Governor's palace / 13. Houses.

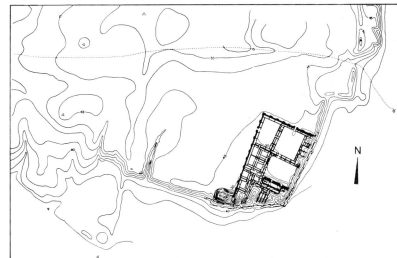

72. *Nineveh, plan of site (from Strommenger, 1963).*

73. *Khorsabad, Portal A of citadel with guardian human-headed winged bulls.*

74. *Khorsabad, guardian human-headed winged bull (detail), from entrance to throne room, palace of Sargon II. Paris, Louvre.*

75. Nimrud, relief from palace, showing fugitives swimming with inflated skins. London, British Museum.

76. Nineveh, relief from palace, showing the sack of the city of Hamanu. London, British Museum.

77. Khorsabad, perspective reconstruction of citadel with palace of Sargon II (from Strommenger, 1963).

78. Khorsabad, perspective reconstruction of city, south from ziggurat (from Strommenger, 1963).

79. Khorsabad, reconstruction of relief, showing the sack of the temple of Musasir by Sargon II (from Strommenger, 1963).

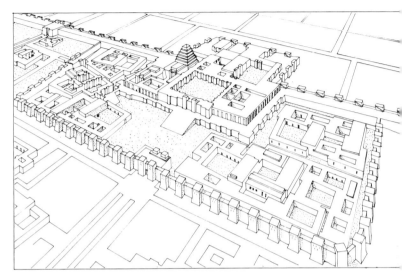

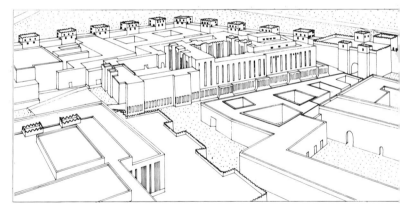

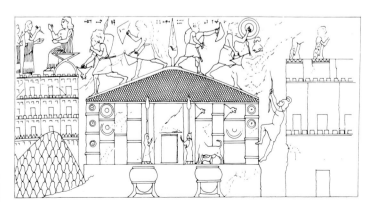

80. Khorsabad, reconstruction of temple façade, Portal Z (from Parrot, 1961).

however, of Sargon's main palace at Khorsabad are more or less comprehensible. The sculptured entrance to a huge public courtyard and the restricted access from this to a slightly smaller "court of honor" recall an arrangement already seen one thousand years earlier in the palace of Mari. The long, rectangular throne room, with its stone emplacement for the throne at one end, is entered through triple doorways, decorated with a composition of sculptures comprising no less than ten winged bulls of varying sizes. Near it is a stairway leading to the flat roof, and behind it, an arrangement of residential and state compartments surrounding a smaller courtyard. Annexed to the palace on the south side is a religious complex consisting of three small temples and a miniature ziggurat, approached by a spiral stairway.

The throne-room unit is repeated on a smaller scale in the minor palaces contained in the lower citadel. As one sees elsewhere, here the architectural planners have failed to profit from the unlimited space available. The buildings are awkwardly disposed and overcrowded. The Nabu temple, which is elevated to the height of the palace platform, has to be connected with it by a stone bridge, under which a street passes. Its plan, on the other hand, like those of the minor palace temples, is typically Late Assyrian. Approached through successive courtyards and vestibules, the sanctuary is entered on its long axis, which terminates in an alcove for the altar.

Something further may be said about Assyrian building construction. The fabric of the city walls consists of mud brick, laid without mortar after the clay had been only partially dried, and solidified by its own weight. The platform at Khorsabad has a heavy facing of dressed stone; stone is used sparingly elsewhere for pavements and the thresholds of important doorways. Kiln-baked bricks are in fairly frequent use, especially for the construction of arches; sometimes they are glazed to create designs in color for facade ornament. Interior wall faces in important chambers, like the throne room at Khorsabad, are covered above the stone reliefs with mural paintings, usually in formal designs. One such design, found in the lower citadel at Khorsabad, has been reconstructed. More freely figured mural paintings from minor Assyrian palaces at Til Barsip and Arslan Tash are now in the Louvre. These more closely reproduce the subjects of the stone reliefs, for which they were substitutes.

Much also has been learned about doors through the discovery in a country palace near Nimrud of the famous Balawat gates. Mounted on a sub-pavement pivot stone and secured by a stone ring at the top, each gate is of wood, decorated with closely spaced horizontal bands of bronze. Though no more than ten inches high, these bands are ornamented in repoussé technique with miniature reliefs depicting in narrative from the campaigns of Shalmaneser III. They are annotated with cuneiform inscriptions and so once more constitute a priceless archaeological document. As for the buildings themselves, most architectural reconstructions are based on the assumption that only flat timber roofs were used; since no windows have

43

82. *Til Barsip,* mural painting from
Assyrian palace. Paris, Louvre.

83,84. *Balawat, Bronze Gates*
(details). London, British Museum.

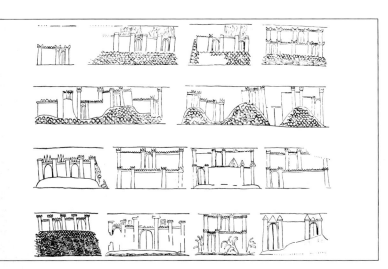

85. Balawat, drawings of fortifications, in Bronze Gates (from Naumann, 1955).

86. Nineveh, relief from palace of Sennacherib, showing Sennacherib at the capitulation of Lakish. London, British Museum.

87. Balawat, Bronze Gates (detail): Assyrian warriors; prisoners brought from Sugunia. London, British Museum.

88. Balawat, Bronze Gates (detail): Assyrian warriors; massacre of prisoners. London, British Museum.

89. *Balawat, Bronze Gates (detail):*
Assyrian warriors; procession of
women prisoners and animals.
London, British Museum.

90. *Gordion, reconstruction of interior of a megaron (from Lloyd, 1967).*

91. *Pazarli (Phrygia), terra cotta relief, showing ibexes. Ankara, Museum.*

92. *Yasilikaya (Phrygia), "Midas Monument."*

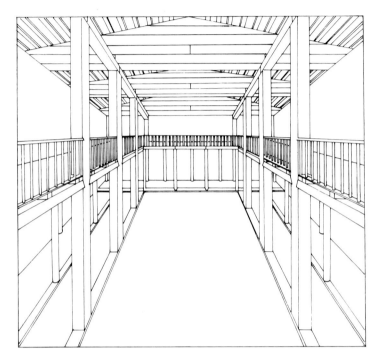

been found, this would occasionally make clerestory lighting possible. The previously mentioned recent discovery at Tell Rimah of elaborate brick vaulting dating from the Old Assyrian period suggests a revision of our ideas on this subject.

The appearance of fortification walls and their gateways is known in part from their excavated remains and in greater detail from their representation in reliefs and on cylinder seals. The tops of the towers rose clear above the connecting walls, and both terminated in crenellated parapets. These projected beyond the wall face beneath, sometimes supported by corbeling or beam-ends, and they were often decorated with an openwork brick pattern. Rectangular windows, real or false, are sometimes shown in the face of the towers. Gateways were flanked by larger towers; the arched entrance between was often decorated with glazed brickwork above the guardian sculptures. The entrance was protected by transverse guardrooms, and a stairway led to the walkway above.

The Phrygians

Little is known about the architecture of Anatolia during the "dark age" that followed the destruction of the Hittite Empire in about 1200 B.C. In this period the plateau was occupied by the Phrygians, but their earliest monuments date only from the ninth and eighth centuries B.C., by which time they had consolidated themselves into a powerful kingdom, with a capital at Gordion on the Sangarius River (now called the Sakarya). Something has been learned about their architecture from excavations made in comparatively recent years. The plans have been recovered of small fortified towns overlying the ruins of larger Hittite cities at such sites as Bogazkoy and Alishar. At Gordion the bastions of an impressive city gate have been brought to light, and in the town itself, public buildings of the megaron type with interesting timber-frame construction. Perhaps even more revealing are the rock-cut monuments of the period, which are concentrated around the principal Phrygian cult center to the southeast of modern Eskishehir. The most striking one is the so-called Midas Monument: a tomb chamber framed in a rock relief representing the gabled facade of a building, whose details are realistically depicted. The building is clearly ornamented with architectural terra cottas and with glazed tiles or figured panels, actual examples of which have been found at other Phrygian sites.

The Urartians

During the final centuries of the Midas dynasty at Gordion the Phrygians were in contact with another newly created nation beyond their eastern frontiers. This was the state of Urartu, which began as a minor kingdom centered on Lake Van, but was later extended by conquest to include not only the eastern provinces of modern Turkey, but some parts of what are

93. Pazarli (Phrygia), terra cotta
relief, showing warriors. Ankara,
Museum.

V. Babylon, reconstruction of Ishtar Gate. Berlin, Museum.

VI. *Pasagarde, tomb of Cyrus II.*

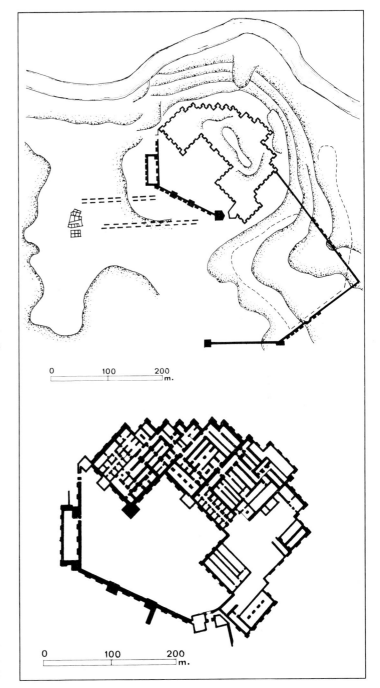

now Soviet Armenia and Iraqi Kurdistan. Interest in the general culture of the Urartians, and particularly in their architecture, has been greatly stimulated by the increasing number of archaeological excavations that have concentrated on Urartian sites in recent years. The results of these excavations create the picture of a prosperous and politically advanced state, which controlled a vast territory of mountainous country. From the ninth to seventh centuries B.C. its actual homeland continued to be the area around Lake Van; but in later years there were widely separated provincial capitals, and between them a well-contrived network of hill fortresses and fortress-cities, connected by good roads and supported by irrigation works. All this, combined with the alpine character of the country in which they lived, served to protect the Urartians from invasion by their neighbors, especially the Assyrians with whom they were continually at war. Their culture was nevertheless based upon that of Mesopotamia, and at one time historians saw in it only a provincial reflection of Assyrian art and architecture. Later discoveries have attributed to it a strong individuality and revealed in its architecture qualities that some consider superior to that of the Assyrians themselves. The monotonous mud-brick facades of the dusty Mesopotamian plain are replaced in Urartu by a pattern of stone towers and battlements adapted to the natural beauty of a rocky landscape.

A dozen of these Urartian fortress-cities have been or are at present being excavated. Built as a rule on a strategic hilltop or mountainside, guarding a pass or river crossing, they have a strong citadel at the summit and a residential walled city on the slopes beneath. Typical examples may be recognized in the ground plans of two provincial cities at sites near Erivan in Soviet Armenia—Karmir Blur and Arin Berd. In the former of these, the staggering of the buttressed wall faces and projecting towers suggests a broken skyline, which must have been architecturally impressive, while the terminal treatment of the battlements, with their crenellated parapets, can be reliably reconstructed on the evidence of a small bronze model of such a building, discovered at another Urartian site, Toprakkale. Prominently placed in most citadel plans is a building recognizable as a temple, a typical example of which may be seen at Altintepe, near Erzincan. The plan is square, with a single compartment enclosed in immensely thick walls and corner buttresses; the centrally placed doorway opens onto a colonnaded courtyard. Early attempts to reconstruct such buildings were usually based on the representation of an Urartian temple facade in an Assyrian relief from Khorsabad. Of the metal facade ornaments shown in this illustration—giant spearheads, circular wall shields, and cauldrons within tripods—actual examples have been found. But where the elevation is concerned, the squat building with its gabled roof is now understood to be the sculptor's misleading adaptation of the shape of the building to the available space. The typical Urartian temple plan is undoubtedly that of a tower, and should be related to the temple towers of Achaemenid times in Persia, for which it clearly provides a prototype. Another public building

51

95. *Toprakkale, bronze model of a building. London, British Museum.*

96. *Toprakkale, bronze model of a building. London, British Museum.*

97. *Altintepe, plan of Urartian temple (from Ozguc, 1966).*
98. *Altintepe, reconstruction of a mural painting.*

at Altintepe, with a roof supported by eighteen internal columns, also foreshadows the basic arrangement of Achaemenian palaces.

The Syro-Hittites

We have seen that in about 1200 B.C. the Hittites were swept from the Anatolian plateau by Phrygian invaders. During the lifetime of the Urartian kingdom, from the tenth to the seventh century B.C., they reappear as part-occupants of several small city-states in northern Syria and the Taurus area. The cities include Carchemish on the Euphrates and others such as Sinjirli and Malatya in the mountains to the northwest, where they shared political authority with indigenous Aramaeans and other peoples. A good deal is known about these Neo- or Syro-Hittites, as they are called, from the results of excavations made early in the present century. Their art and architecture were of a hybrid and slightly inferior character, much influenced in their later days by Assyria, to which the Syro-Hittites frequently became subject, but also by the Phoenicians of Syria and even by Egypt. One notices, above all in their public buildings, the plentiful use of sculptured orthostats, sometimes of coarse black basalt awkwardly alternating with whitish limestone. An innovation is the use of wooden columns with stone capitals and sculptured bases representing paired animals; monolithic statues, more than lifesize, are another common feature.

Syro-Hittite cities vary in shape and size, but they are always well fortified. The walls of Sinjirli enclose an almost perfect circle one-half mile in diameter; in the center is a high, fortified citadel containing a complex of palaces and guardhouses. The citadel at Carchemish is an ancient mound overlooking the Euphrates, and the enceinte of fortress walls has been extended twice. In all these cities the most conspicuous and characteristic features are the palaces built to an architectural formula known to the Assyrians as a *bît-hilani*. We have seen the early development of this formula in buildings of the second millennium B.C. at Tell Atchana. It consists of a columned portico, a long reception room with a staircase beside it leading to the roof, and a varying number of residential or retiring rooms behind. A striking example is the great Kapara palace at Tell Halaf, near the source of the Khabur River. A purely Aramaean dynasty of princes ruled in this city in the ninth century B.C., and they decorated their palace with an almost barbaric array of sculptures, as in the portico columns composed of grotesque human figures and mythical beasts. The construction of Syro-Hittite buildings is usually of mud brick heavily reinforced with timber. An exception to this generalization may be found at Carchemish; and one is reminded that this city lies in an area less subject to earthquakes.

The Levant

Syro-Hittite monuments have been found as far south as Hama on the upper course of the Orontes. Here, in Syria, the Hittites are known to have been in contact with the Biblical Israelites; they must also have had trading

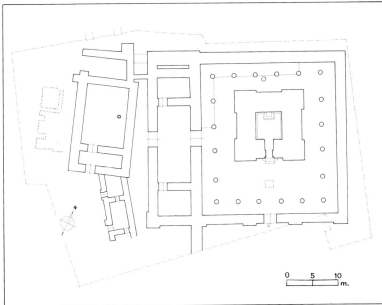

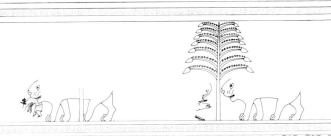

99. *Carchemish, plan of city*
(from Akurgal, 1962).

100,101. *Carchemish, wall relief*
with funeral cortege (details).
London, British Museum.

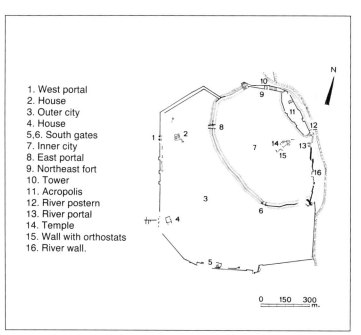

1. West portal
2. House
3. Outer city
4. House
5,6. South gates
7. Inner city
8. East portal
9. Northeast fort
10. Tower
11. Acropolis
12. River postern
13. River portal
14. Temple
15. Wall with orthostats
16. River wall.

102. Carchemish, relief on
orthostat, showing King Katuwas.
London, British Museum.

103. Carchemish, seated statue
on base of paired lions. London,
British Museum.

104. *Sinjirli, plan of city (from Akurgal, 1962).*

105. *Sinjirli, plan of citadel (from Akurgal, 1962).*

106. *Sinjirli, wall construction, showing interior "paneling" (from Naumann, 1955).*

107. *Tell Tayanat, carved column base of palace.*

108. *Tell Tayanat, isometric diagram of palace and temple (from Frankfort, 1954).*

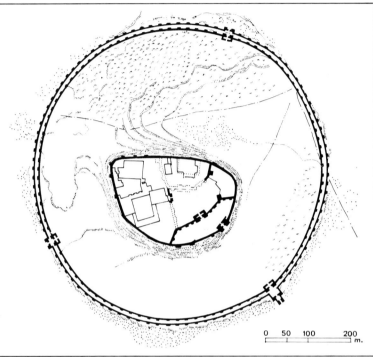

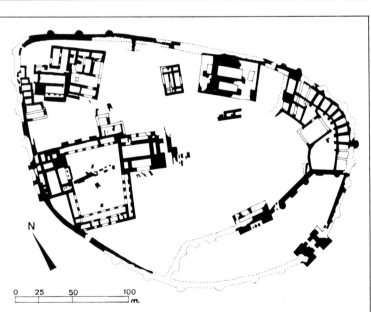

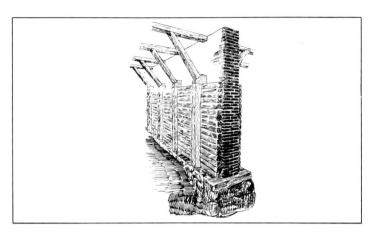

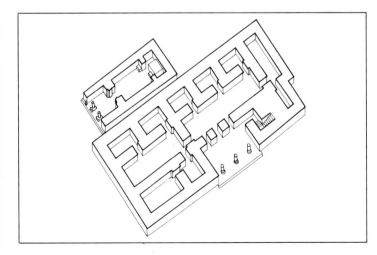

relations with the Phoenicians, a Canaanite people whose homeland was a strip of the Levant coast reaching from Tartus to south of Mount Carmel. Our knowledge of both Phoenician and Israelite architecture is derived from excavations in Syria and Palestine, which for the most part have been concerned with fortified cities. A close study has been made of historical development in the design of city walls and gateways. One of the earliest examples, with a stone glacis and moat, has been exposed at Hazor in Galilee, and dates from the eighteenth century B.C. By the time of King Solomon, in the tenth century, military architecture of this sort seems to have been standardized, for at three cities—Hazor, Megiddo, and Gezer—walls and gates alike are almost identical. Walls are of the casemate type, with internal chambers for storage or the accommodation of the garrison. Gateways have become elaborate structures, their entry protected by flanking towers and consisting of three successive transverse chambers, to each of which in turn the attackers would need to gain access. It is thought that in the ninth century B.C. a new and improved battering ram must have been invented, against which the casemate wall proved an inadequate defense. It was accordingly replaced by a solid wall of equal thickness, sometimes with salients and recesses to give it greater stability.

Such remains as have been found of Canaanite temples date mostly from the late second millennium and are not very informative. Examples found at Hazor and elsewhere give at least an idea of the temple plan, which consists of a courtyard, main hall, and sanctuary, all on a single axis, with occasional side chambers. This convention must have survived at least into the tenth century B.C., because it is recognizable in the Biblical description of Solomon's Temple, which was built by Phoenician craftsmen. A well-known though not altogether convincing reconstruction of this building shows the three main compartments surrounded by narrow side chambers in three stories. On either side of the central doorway are the pair of "brazen pillars" mentioned in the Bible, a feature that also appears in the Hazor temple.

The Neo-Babylonian Period

One final chapter in the history of Mesopotamian architecture now remains to be studied. After the fall of Nineveh in 612 B.C. and the subsequent collapse of the Assyrian Empire, the center of power shifted from the upper Tigris to the lower Euphrates, and the city of Babylon was rebuilt on a magnificent scale by the kings of a Neo-Babylonian dynasty. Herodotus, who is thought to have visited Babylon in or about 460 B.C., said, "It surpasses in splendor any city of the known world"; and the long description of it that he wrote is interesting to compare with the results of the German excavations of 1899-1917. The excavations show that Herodotus' account of the fortifications at least was not greatly exaggerated. The inner city is an irregular rectangle with a perimeter of almost exactly five miles, divided into two unequal parts by the bed of the

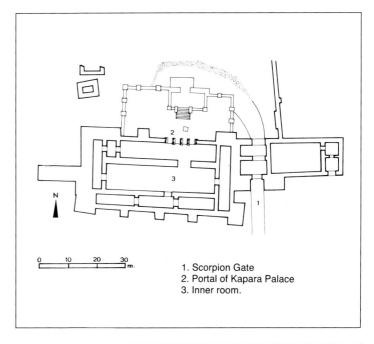

1. Scorpion Gate
2. Portal of Kapara Palace
3. Inner room.

111. Tell Halaf, reconstruction
of portico, Kapara Palace. Berlin,
Museum.

VII. Persepolis, apadana.

VIII. *Persepolis, apadana columns.*

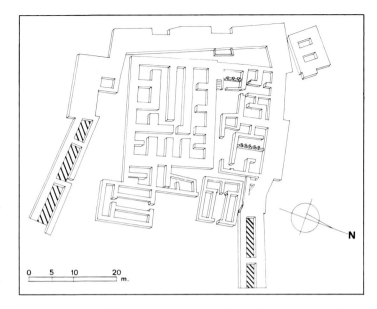

Euphrates. The eastern part alone, on which the German archaeologists concentrated their attention, slightly exceeds in area Sargon's Khorsabad. It was defended by a double wall, with pairs of towers at intervals of sixty-five feet, and by a navigable moat connected to the river. The moat was spanned by bridges leading to the six main gates. Nebuchadnezzar greatly extended the area of the city by building a triangular outer wall five miles long. This also had a moat, but the space between the double walls was filled with rubble to support a broad walkway behind the parapets. The main approach to the city was from the north, by a broad street known to us as the Processional Way; the entrance to the inner city was through the Ishtar Gate, a magnificent building that has been reconstructed in the Berlin Museum. Continuing southward, the stone-paved street skirted the broad temenos enclosure with its colossal ziggurat, Etemenanki; then, turning westward between these buildings and the "low" temple, Esagila, it crossed the river on a stone bridge to the western quarter of the town. The remainder of the inner city was filled with minor temples and large private houses, some of them terraced into the sides of the substantial mound, called Merkez, which represented the remains of earlier cities. The Ishtar Gate was an elaborate construction, with four towers and a huge rectangular gatehouse. Its facades and those of the Processional Way were faced with bricks covered in colored glaze and figured with lions, bulls, and mythical animals, mostly molded in relief. The labor of casting each brick in its appropriate wooden mold can be imagined, but the effect of these brilliant colors, in contrast to the ubiquitous mud brick of the surrounding city, must have been very striking. Of these buildings, all that remains today in situ are the foundations, which, according to some ritual formula, were carried down some twenty feet below pavement level in search of "clean" soleil. They too are decorated with figures in relief, but are unglazed because they were not intended to be seen.

Curiously enough, the two buildings that the excavators were least able to reconstruct with any assurance were the ziggurat and the huge temple of Babylon's patron god, Marduk. The ziggurat had been almost completely quarried by brick robbers, while Esagila was buried beneath an almost impenetrable burden of later building remains. More completely excavated was Nebuchadnezzar's great palace to the west of the Ishtar Gate. Entered from the Processional Way, it is planned around at least four main courtyards. The throne room itself faces the third of these, with three doorways and a recess for the throne opposite the center door. The outer facade between the doorways was once more decorated with glazed bricks, and the designs here remind one that contact had by now been made between Mesopotamia and Classical Greece. Between the second and third courts there is a high-standing propylon, which recalls the reception unit of an Assyrian palace. A building in the northeast corner, comprising heavily vaulted storerooms, has been tentatively identified as an emplacement for the Hanging Gardens of classical tradition.

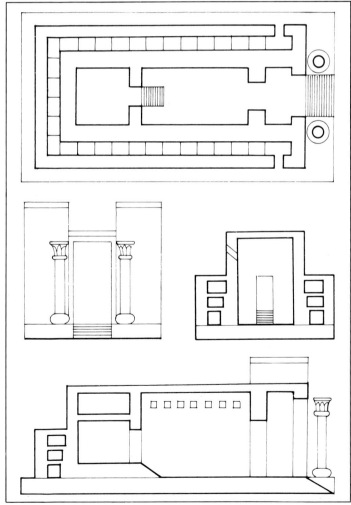

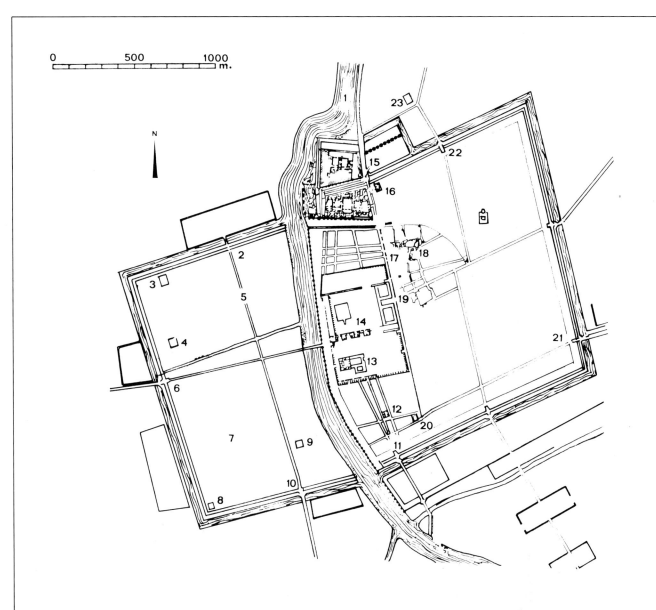

0   500   1000
m.

N

1. Euphrates River / 2. Lugalgirra Gate / 3. Temple of Belit Nina / 4. Temple of Adad / 5. Gardens / 6. Adad Gate / 7. New Town /
8. Mausoleum / 9. Temple of Shamash / 10. Shamash Gate / 11. Urash Gate / 12. Temple of Gula / 13. Temple of Marduk /
14. Esagila / 15. Ishtar Gate / 16. Temple of Nin-Makh / 17. Processional Way / 18. Temple of Ishtar / 19. Sacred Gate /
20. Temple of Ninurta / 21. Ninurta Gate / 22. Sin Gate / 23. Temple of New Year Festival.

IX. *Persepolis, apadana, detail of the exterior ramp.*

X. *Persepolis, apadana, interior relief of the east staircase.*

115. *Babylon, perspective reconstruction of city (from Parrot, 1961).*

116. *Babylon, perspective
reconstruction of Ishtar Gate and
Processional Way (from Parrot,
1961).*

117. *Babylon, line reconstruction
of Ishtar Gate (from Strommenger,
1963).*

118. *Babylon, reconstruction of
Ishtar Gate. Berlin, Museum.*

119. *Babylon, plan of Nin-Makh
Temple (from Strommenger, 1963).*

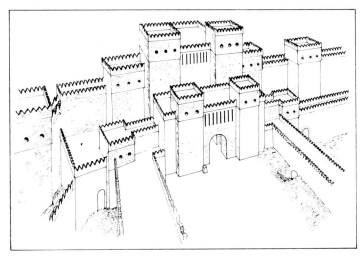

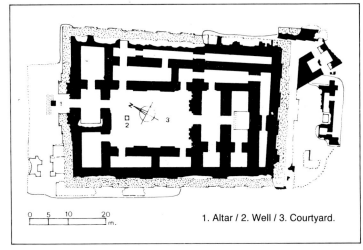

1. Altar / 2. Well / 3. Courtyard.

120. *Babylon, plan of the Great Palace (from Strommenger, 1963).*

121. *Babylon, plan of largest private house (from Macqueen, 1964).*

122. *Babylon, glazed brick facade of throne room from palace of Nebuchadnezzar. Berlin, Museum.*

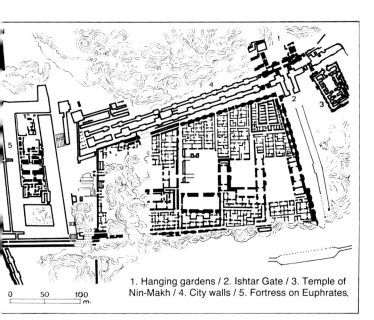

1. Hanging gardens / 2. Ishtar Gate / 3. Temple of Nin-Makh / 4. City walls / 5. Fortress on Euphrates.

0   50   100
m.

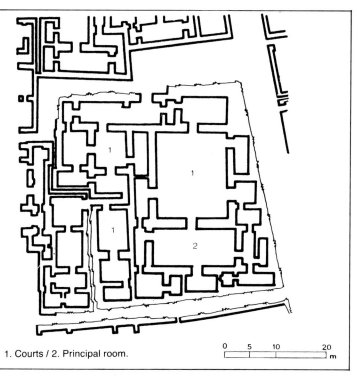

1. Courts / 2. Principal room.

0   5   10   20
m

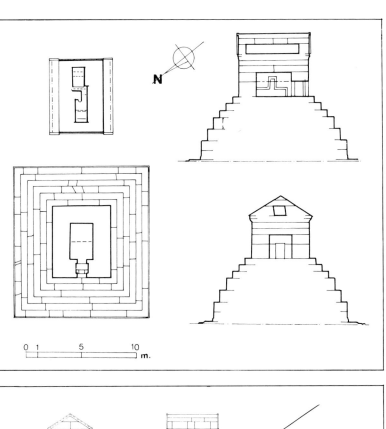

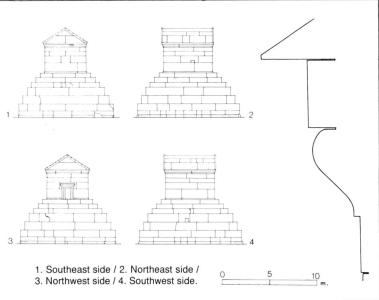

1. Southeast side / 2. Northeast side /
3. Northwest side / 4. Southwest side.

Little reference has till now been made to the architecture of private houses. At Babylon the ruins of some impressively large ones have been examined, but there is little to be said about them that does not equally apply to ordinary dwellings dating from any period in the history of the ancient Near East. For security reasons, there are no windows in their blank external facades, so that light must be obtained from open courtyards or roofed courts with clerestory openings. A main reception room, entered laterally from a court, is the most obvious feature; in early houses at Ur, Woolley detected evidence of a wooden gallery around this court, suggesting the existence of an upper story. Nothing of this sort was found at Babylon, which suggests that Herodotus' account was in this respect at fault. The planning of such houses was often hampered by the irregular shape of the site available in a frequently rebuilt crowded quarter. This fact has some relevance to the subject of Mesopotamian town planning in general, about which no scholar has ever ventured to write at any great length. To be truthful, planning as we know it today—that is, the conscious design and disposal of buildings in relation to each other—was practically nonexistent in the cities of the ancient Near East. Apart from private dwellings, the public buildings themselves were designed, as it were, from the inside outward, and little thought seems to have been given to their interrelation or overall composition. We have seen, for example, the citadel at Khorsabad, the palace platform at Nimrud, and the walled city of Ur, with their individual palaces and temples placed haphazard in apparently unrelated positions. Except for the Processional Way at Babylon, it would be hard to find any trace of a preplanned civic layout of the sort that becomes familiar in later times. Such things had to await the advent of Greek influence, which after the final conquest of Mesopotamian lands by the Persians soon began to be in greater evidence.

ACHAEMENIAN ARCHITECTURE

The development and history of Mesopotamian architecture must be considered to end with the conquest of Babylon by Cyrus the Great in 539 B.C. Some account must now be given of subsequent events in Persia under the Achaemenid dynasty, of which Cyrus was the founder. With this purpose in view, it will be well first to recollect the historical background against which Achaemenian art and architecture came into being. The country that we now call Iran had for some centuries been withdrawn from the mainstream of cultural development in the Near East. Its most recent rulers were the Medes, whose tribal dispensation had afforded little encouragement to the refinements of civilization. Now, with the sudden elevation of the Persians to an imperial power and the sweeping success of their conquests, an unprecedented situation had been created. It was as though civilization had suddenly fallen to a tribe of seminomadic horsemen, who were in a position either to accept or to destroy the cultural

125. Pasargadae, tomb of Cyrus II.

126. *Pasargadae, residential palace, from southwest.*

127. *Choga Zambil, perspective reconstruction of ziggurat (from Strommenger, 1963).*

128. *Persepolis, general view, from east: foreground, Hall of One Hundred Columns (throne hall of Xerxes); behind, audience hall of Darius I (apadana); left, tripylon.*

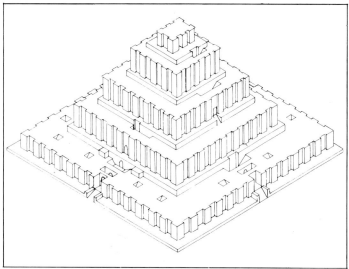

129. *Persepolis, plan of site (from Frankfort, 1954).*

130. *Persepolis, north staircase of audience hall of Darius (apadana), front view of outer ramps.*

131. *Persepolis, palace of Xerxes, from northeast.*

132. *Persepolis, reconstruction of Hall of One Hundred Columns (throne hall of Xerxes) (from Frankfort, 1954).*

133. *Persepolis, audience hall of Darius (apadana), ramps of north staircase.* ▷

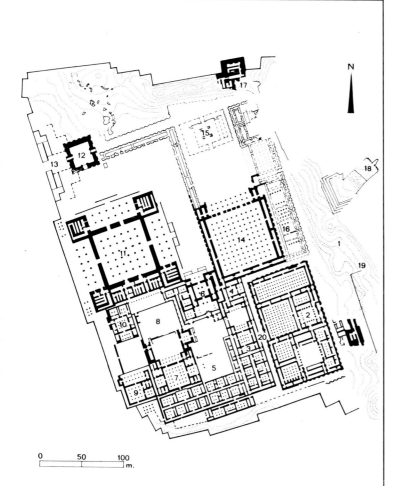

1. East fortifications / 2. Treasury / 3. Harem / 4. Guard room / 5. Ruined buildings / 6. Tripylon / 7. Palace of Xerxes / 8. Ruined buildings / 9. Unidentified palace / 10. Palace of Darius / 11. Audience hall of Darius / 12. Gate house of Xerxes / 13. Staircase to terrace / 14. Throne hall of Xerxes (Hall of One Hundred Columns) / 15. Gate to court of throne hall / 16. Outbuildings / 17. North fortifications / 18. Royal tomb / 19. Cistern / 20. Street between harem and treasury.

134. *Persepolis, reliefs showing bearers of gifts, on north staircase to audience hall of Darius (apadana).*

135. *Persepolis, relief showing lion attacking a bull, on staircase to tripylon.*

136. *Susa, glazed brick reliefs: archer of royal guard. Paris, Louvre.*

137. *Persepolis, bull capital (detail).*

heritage they had acquired. Certainly, where architecture was concerned, the Persians not only accepted this heritage but enhanced it with their own peculiar genius.

The earliest stages in the evolution of Achaemenian architecture are to be seen in the rather scanty remains of Cyrus' capital city at Pasargadae. The style is understandably derivative, combining Median and Urartian with Assyrian elements. The layout still retains the character of a nomadic encampment: widely separated buildings—consisting of gatehouse, residential palace, and audience hall—standing in a vast park, surrounded by a wall thirteen feet thick. Only the audience hall provides an example of a formula in design later to become a criterion of Achaemenian architecture: a hypostyle hall with corner towers and external colonnades between them, called by the Persians an apadana.

The full flower of Achaemenian architecture is to be seen at Persepolis, to which Darius transferred the state capital in 518 B.C. Two new sources of influence are now in evidence. One is the traditional architecture of Elam, which had thrived from the second millennium B.C. onward and whose true character has only recently been revealed by the excavation of a great ziggurat and temple complex at Choga Zambil. The other—a far more significant development—is the knowledge of Greek architecture and the great army of Greek craftsmen that Darius had brought back from his wars in the Aegean. It is to these influences, combined with the creative talent of the Persians themselves, that the truly novel features of Achaemenian architecture must be attributed. Its links with the past on the other hand were supplied by Mesopotamia. Achaemenian palaces, like those of Assyria, were built on artificial terraces; their gates were guarded by winged demons and human-headed bulls; their walls were built of mud brick and decorated with panels of polychrome glazed tiles or relief sculptures in stone. But in other ways, striking innovations may be recognized in the lavish use of wooden columns with elaborately carved stone capitals, in the sculptured stone frames of doors and windows, in the monumental stairways ornamented with figured reliefs, and in the tendency to plan important buildings around a square central unit.

At Persepolis the most striking effects of Greek craftsmanship, imposed on the native tradition of Persian art, are best seen in the sculptured reliefs themselves, whose major contribution to the appearance of the buildings is immediately apparent. The straightforward relief technique of the Assyrians, with its engraved detail and lack of modeling, has been retained as a basis for the new style, but the employment of Ionian sculptors results in a complete break with Mesopotamian tradition. Relief carving in Assyria had maintained until the end its linear character, with modeling playing a very subordinate part; the surface of the figures stood in front of the background as in a parallel plane, almost without three-dimensional treatment. These limitations were distasteful to the Greek sculptors, for

whom sculpture in the round and sculpture in relief were closely related, so that a fuller plastic rendering of human and animal subjects now became the rule. In the Greek manner, it is carried to extremes in the modeling of drapery, through which are perceptible the contours of the body. The outcome of these innovations produces a form of sculpture whose elegance and precision is probably unrivaled in the whole history of art. If any criticism is to be made of the Persepolis reliefs, it is in regard not to the details of the carving, but to the poverty of imagination in the subjects depicted. The interminable processions of almost identical figures tend to become monotonous, and one remembers by contrast the spirit and variety of the Assyrian narrative scenes. However, these Persian reliefs fulfill a totally different function in the decoration of a building: the Assyrian palace reliefs were used internally and confront the spectator at close quarters, whereas the Persian reliefs are used as ornament for the outside facades of artificial terraces on which the buildings stood. Dominated by the walls and roofs above, which have now disappeared, they were intended merely to give decorative emphasis to the most important external features of the architecture—the stairway approaches to the palaces.

If we now consider individual buildings on the palace platform at Persepolis, we shall find the great apadana of Darius obviously the most impressive. It is 250 feet square with a height computed at fifty feet, and it is said to have accommodated ten thousand people. The towers at each of the four corners may have contained guardrooms and stairs. From the western portico there was an open view of the countryside, and perhaps also of the sunset in the evening, since a low parapet here replaced the fortress wall that surrounded the rest of the terrace. The private terrace on which the apadana stood was cut from living rock, and the great stairways leading up to it bore the famous reliefs of tribute bearers. Next comes the throne hall or Hall of One Hundred Columns, begun by Xerxes and finished by Artaxerxes I. The portico on its north side was supported by sixteen pillars and had at either end two huge guardian figures of bulls, which were built into the walls of the towers. The wall between hall and portico contained seven stone window frames; the short walls had niches instead of windows. The reveals of the doorways were also carved in relief.

The identity of the majority of other buildings on the main terrace is hypothetical. The "Harem" is to some extent self-explanatory, while the character of the "Treasury" is evident in the fact that it is accessible only through a single small doorway. In common with all these buildings, its columns were of wood, heavily plastered and painted in bright colors. They are fluted in the Classical Greek manner, while the more elaborate bases and capitals show a floral treatment that is half Greek and half Egyptian. Examples have been found at Persepolis and elsewhere of the double-figure impost block (bulls, bullmen, or dragons), a feature that is peculiar to Achaemenian architecture.

XI. Persepolis, palace of Xerxes, sculpture in the portico.

Architecture of Egypt / Hans Wolfgang Müller

138. *Hieroglyphs representing*
primitive forms of Egyptian temples
a, b) from Petrie, 1901; c) from
Lauer, 1935; d, e) from Davies,
1900-1901.

THE PREDYNASTIC PERIOD

Egyptian architecture did not develop from homogeneous principles and traditions. Upper and Lower Egypt remained geographically and culturally distinct, even when joined politically in the Kingdom of the Two Lands. They had different peoples with their own customs, characteristic dwellings, and modes of burial, with different ideas about the divine powers and about the kind of life that followed death. In both regions the cultivation and storage of crops had long been the basis of existence. Settled farmers tend to build permanent dwellings with provision for their grain, cattle, and tools, but in Upper Egypt the farmers shared the land with a nomadic people who had migrated to the Nile Valley from the increasingly arid steppes. Hunters and herdsmen, roaming to find well-stocked hunting grounds and fresh pastures, have always built dwellings that are easily erected and taken down wherever they choose to camp; thus these lived in lightweight tentlike structures with roofs and walls of skins or matting stretched over a rigid frame.

Each region also had its own distinctive burial practices. The inhabitants of Upper Egypt, to the south, buried their dead away from the settlements, in the dry sand at the edge of the nearby desert, and formed a mound or tumulus over the grave. The deceased had to be provided with everything they might need—weapons, adornments, food and drink—for their continued separate existence. But in the north, in Lower Egypt, which was flat and wet, the dead received the protection of the villages on higher ground, and were buried under the floor of the houses; thus they remained within the sphere of the living. Each of these modes of burial presented a different conception of the nature of the afterlife and of the necessary ritual provisions for a continued existence.

Even in Predynastic times the typical settler lived in a rectangular one-room peasant hut of sun-dried Nile mud. A model of such a hut, found in a tomb, plainly shows the inward sloping walls, the door, and the tiny window openings set high for ventilation more than to let in light. The roof has not survived, but it was flat and may originally have consisted of palm trunks laid side by side: this type of roof was sculpturally reproduced on the ceilings of later stone-built tombs. The slope of the walls later became a characteristic feature of monumental stone architecture: tombs, temples, gate towers (pylons), and enclosure walls. It goes back to the early architectural experience with primitive mud-walled structures.

From the very beginning the inhabitants of the Nile Valley and the Delta had made shelters and huts from reeds and rushes. Reeds and papyrus stems, tied or woven together to form walls and bundled together to form light supports for the roofing, are the oldest building materials in Egypt. Ancient hieroglyphs represent various types of huts in simplified outline. These huts made of perishable material, together with the primitive mud houses, served as prototypes for the later monumental architecture. In

a) Lower Egyptian sanctuary of the goddess Neith of Sais (First Dynasty) / b) Buto heron sanctuary (Narmer mace, Hierakonpolis, First Dynasty) / c) Upper Egyptian sanctuary (after Third Dynasty hieroglyph) / d) Lower Egyptian sanctuary (after Fifth Dynasty hieroglyph) / e) Reed hut beneath awning (after Fifth Dynasty hieroglyph).

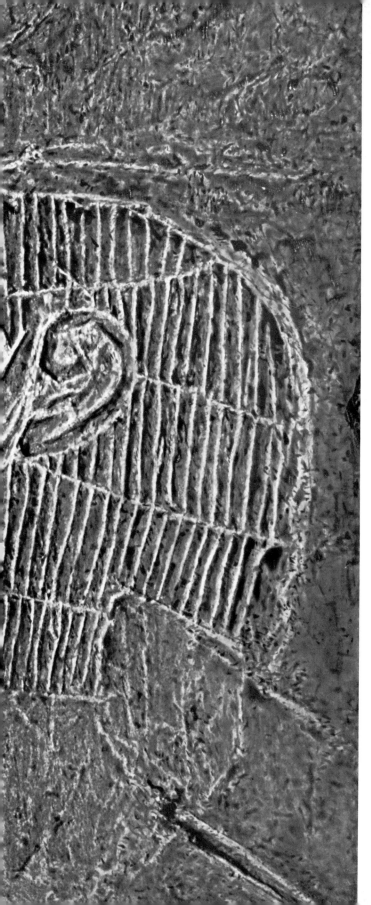

139. *Walled Lower Egyptian city, from Palette of Menes (Narmer). Unification period, c. 3000 B.C. Cairo, Egyptian Museum.*

140. *Abydos, funerary stele with the "Horus name" of King Zet; below, representation of palace facade. First Dynasty, c. 2900 B.C. Paris, Louvre.*

141. *Abydos, reconstruction of royal tumulus tomb with steles. First Dynasty (from Lauer, 1955).*

142. *Abydos, plan of temple of Khentiamentiu. First Dynasty (from Smith, 1958).*

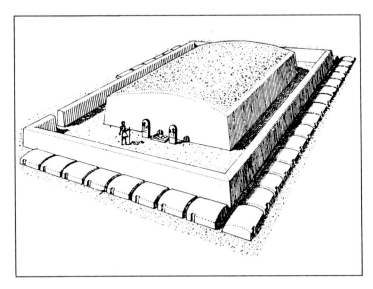

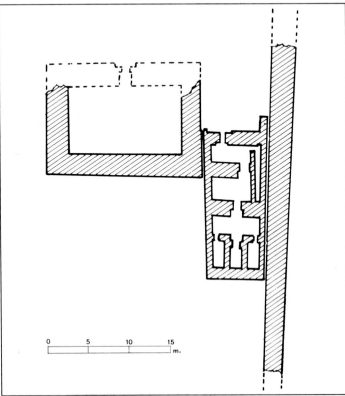

hieroglyphic writing the two "royal sanctuaries" of Upper and Lower Egypt are distinguished by huts of two kinds. A hut with a semicircular roof, above which two corner posts appear to project, must be interpreted as a structure consisting of bundled reeds and matting on the basis of its green or yellow color in the writing. In the oldest representations this hut form also denotes the holy places of Buto, the capital of a prehistoric Delta kingdom; in the writing, the "royal sanctuary of Lower Egypt." Translated into three dimensions, this type of hut reveals its basic structure: a building with a roof vaulted longitudinally, between elevated transverse walls.

The reed hut of Lower Egypt corresponded to the Upper Egyptian tent of the nomad chieftain, a frame building designed to resemble an animal, with horns projecting from the front and sometimes a fence around the main entrance; at the back hung down an animal tail. The imprints of ancient cylinder seals have transmitted this aboriginal building type; in the developed hieroglyphic writing the animal features have been toned down. The nomad chieftains, who first brought the two kingdoms under their own rule and created the united Egyptian state, had long been settled in the Nile Valley but continued to live in tents, stretching colored matting over the structural skeletons. After Memphis was founded as the permanent residence of the kings of Upper and Lower Egypt, the palace of reed matting remained a model for the palace of the king as ruler of Upper Egypt and for the shrines of Upper Egyptian gods; but it was now constructed—like the reed hut, its Lower Egyptian equivalent—of solid brick and timber. Both of these building types testified to their particular origins and significance within the new political order, and accordingly their characteristic structural features had to be strictly preserved in the more permanent monumental form.

Another building type known from hieroglyphs was also composed of vegetable material. The tall rectangular front of this hut was of matting construction with the corners and eaves stiffened and reinforced with bundles of plant stems bound together. The concave cornice, highly stylized, probably represents the free ends of the rushes that tied the upper edges of the matting walls to the top stiffener. As a hieroglyph this hut means "hut of the god," and in monumental architecture it is perpetuated in the exterior design of a chapel held together with round fillets and crowned by a concave cornice. In the older writing it also appears in another special form, namely, a hut beneath an awning supported on wooden posts. In monumental architecture this form became the prototype of the later "baldachin temple," erected for the celebration of special rites and as a "way station" or resting-place for the images of the gods and their sacred barge during the processions through the precincts of large temple complexes. The "birth houses" of the late temples were also modeled after the hut shaded by an awning.

143. *North Saqqara, reconstruction of tomb of Queen Herneith (from Lauer, 1955).*

144. *North Saqqara, "Buto tomb" with elaborate niche articulation. First Dynasty, c. 2900 B.C.*

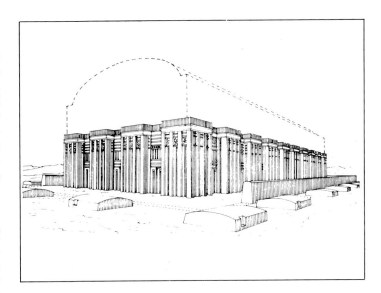

THE THINITE PERIOD AND THE OLD KINGDOM

Menes (Narmer), who unified Upper and Lower Egypt, built his residence in Lower Egypt on the site where later the capital city of Memphis was erected. The name of the palace, "white walls," suggests a brick enclosure, and within it were the residences of the king, the shrines of the gods, and the government buildings of the Two Lands, all these in the styles of Upper and Lower Egypt, respectively. Walls reinforced with projecting buttresses were characteristic of the conquered Lower Egyptian cities, as seen in representations of the triumphs of Menes (Narmer), this Lower Egyptian tradition being adopted by the conqueror from Upper Egypt for his stronghold in the Delta.

The Palace Facade

In the combination of the two different building forms—the tent palace of the Upper Egyptian king and the niched enclosure wall of his Lower Egyptian residence—is an artistic translation of the "Horus name" that thenceforth constitutes the first part of the royal title for the united Egypt: within an upright rectangle is enclosed an artfully composed facade with two gates, the whole surmounted by the ruler as the Horus-hawk. Preserved painted representations of decorative matting and wood framing on the projecting and recessed faces of these articulated walls have been taken as evidence that their niche-modeled surface was derived from wood construction—and from Mesopotamia, where contemporary finds include similar buildings depicted on cylinder seals. However, subsequent monuments make it clear that the wall articulated with niches belongs to a quite different mode of construction from the matting stretched over a wood frame; both were purely Egyptian in origin and, heraldically merged in the "palace name," came together in the Memphis residence. A better idea of what Upper and Lower Egypt contributed to the building forms in and around the royal residence can be obtained from the tombs that were built by the unifiers of the country and their successors, especially the limestone tomb precinct of King Zoser.

The unification of Upper and Lower Egypt stimulated the development of a true architecture with quite new tasks, and foremost among these was the building of monumental tombs for the kings of the unified country. Toward the end of the Predynastic period the wood frame for molded mud brick was invented, which was a technical step forward.

Tomb Complexes of the Early Kings

The form of tomb structures grows from the dual nature of the Egyptian kings as "rulers of Upper and Lower Egypt"; this required two separate burials, one in each half of the country. The prehistoric burial customs that had evolved—cemetery burial in a tumulus grave in Upper Egypt and house burial in Lower Egypt—were incorporated into the architecture of

the royal tomb complexes. In Memphis the Lower Egyptian idea of house burial led logically to the tomb being designed and equipped as a "residence"; in the Upper Egyptian cemetery at Abydos, on the other hand, the grave mounds were merely enlarged and developed into abstract geometric shapes. The cult arrangements within each mode of burial led also to particular formations.

The Royal Cemetery at Abydos

At Abydos the subterranean burial chambers of the royal tumuli were walled with brick, the floors and walls faced with imported softwoods, and the burial pit roofed over with timbers. However it is known that during the First Dynasty one of these tombs was given a floor and walls of granite blocks that herald the transition to a stone architecture. The tumulus, a heap of sand, rose above the timbered roof that covered the tomb chamber and the lateral rooms for grave furniture; it was contained by a brick wall and probably covered by a shallow brick dome. In front of the east side of the tumulus two freestanding name steles were set up to indicate the offering place. The entire precinct was surrounded by a low wall, outside of which the members of the king's family and court were interred. The royal cemetery, which lies in flat desert country about a mile from the Nile Valley, stood under the protection of Khentiamentiu ("Foremost of the Westerners"), a god of the dead who had a temple at the edge of the valley. This was a brick building whose foundations are preserved, the only example of an Early Dynastic temple. It was elongated in plan; on the short side, two outer chambers with offset entrances led into a third room where the shrine for the cult image was built against the rear wall. As the oldest representations show, the shrine was originally a construction of reeds standing free within an enclosure; when translated into brick it became solidly incorporated in the structure of a closed building, and was moved back against the rear wall.

The Royal Tombs at Memphis

The first rulers of the united country and their successors, as kings of Lower Egypt, lie buried on the western desert plateau across from their capital at Memphis; their tombs are of a type adapted from the burial practices of Buto, once the capital of a Lower Egyptian kingdom. These Memphite tombs have imposing mud-brick superstructures whose multi-layered exteriors form a series of buttresses and niches. They demonstrate the Lower Egyptian palace in the characteristic aspect of its articulated enclosure walls. The articulation has now become an aesthetic system: on the projecting and recessed faces are painted colorful carpet patterns that link the idea of the tomb as a "Lower Egyptian residence" with that of the tent palace derived from Upper Egypt, and thus symbolically express for each king the guaranty of the unified kingdom. The "palace tombs" are also surrounded by low walls, and outside these, as at Abydos, the subsidiary

graves are ranged. The offering place of the palace tomb was located in front of a niche in the exterior of the east wall. Detached from its structural context, this niche later became incorporated as a "false door" in the royal and private tombs of the Old Kingdom, a Lower Egyptian element symbolically linking the worlds of the living and the dead. In this isolation of its form and function the false door is frequently edged with beading and crowned by a concave molding. It persisted in three-dimensional or in painted form into the later dynasties and even found its way into temples and palaces, occurring wherever a deceased person, a god, or the king was to appear.

King Zoser's Funerary Precinct at Memphis

To revitalize and consolidate the idea of a unified kingdom, King Zoser, the founder of the Third Dynasty, combined the two separate cemeteries and their funerary institutions into a single giant precinct near his capital of Memphis. The sanctuary was surrounded by niched walls of white limestone over thirty feet high; these represented the "white walls" of the residence. At the focal point of the entire precinct stands the 200-foot stepped tomb, combining an exaggerated monumental stone tumulus in the Upper Egyptian tradition (mastaba) with the idea of a gigantic stairway to heaven. It is still possible to distinguish the various stages in the history of this structure—from the original flat mastaba to a small pyramid, then to the final large step pyramid. The king's Lower Egyptian tomb is a massive stone structure attached to the south wall of the sanctuary; its arched cornice and niched facade correspond to the royal tombs of the unifiers at Memphis. In a consistent development of the Lower Egyptian-Memphite concept of the "house tomb," the other buildings within the precinct are patterned after the Memphis residence, including the king's palace, the government buildings of the Two Lands, and the shrines of Upper and Lower Egyptian gods. In the courts of the tomb complex the royal existence in the hereafter was affirmed and perpetually renewed by ritual reenactments of the "jubilee festival" in the presence of the gods.

The various building types in King Zoser's burial precinct were shown three-dimensionally in stone in their Upper and Lower Egyptian forms, with architectural elements appropriately painted for their cult requirements. Airy wood-framed structures covered with reed matting in the nomadic manner of Upper Egypt are recognizable by their arched roofs, fluted masts, and the mats stretched between cross battens or rolled up over doorways. The Lower Egyptian chapels reproduce the forms of the ancient hut of bundled and woven reeds; as independent decorative elements, the round fillet and concave upper molding have their origin in the translation of primeval reed forms into stone. Brick buildings are identifiable from the flat roof and interior ceiling construction, which simulates round timbers resting on architraves supported by fluted wooden posts. Wooden door leaves are reproduced in stone in a half-open position.

146. *Saqqara, mortuary precinct of King Zoser, re-erected enclosure wall with niche articulation and step pyramid. Third Dynasty, c. 2650 B.C.*

147. *Saqqara, plan of mortuary precinct of King Zoser (from Lange-Hirmer, 1957).*

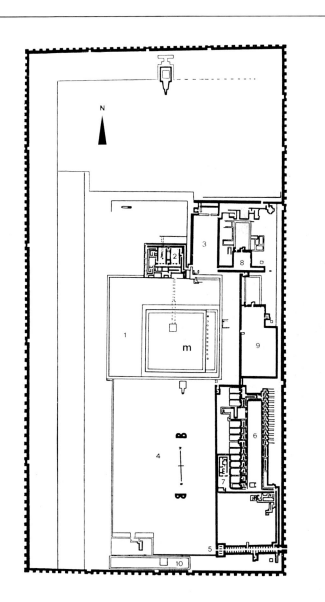

1. Step pyramid derived from square-plan mastaba / 2. Funerary temple of Zoser / 3. Court with Serdah / 4. Large court with altar on two B-shaped stones / 5. Entrance portico / 6. Heb-Sed court / 7. Small temple / 8. Court before South Palace / 9. Court of South Palace / 10. South tomb.

148. *Saqqara, mortuary precinct of King Zoser, reconstruction of Upper Egyptian tent building for the government of Lower Egypt (from Lauer, 1955).*

149. *Saqqara, mortuary precinct of King Zoser, remains of Upper Egyptian tent building for the government of Lower Egypt.*

150. *Saqqara, mortuary precinct of King Zoser, detail of building for government of Lower Egypt: fluted masts, stretched matting in lower section, entrance with rolled-up mats. Third Dynasty, c. 2650 B.C.*

The fluting of the posts as an artistic form probably goes back to the dressing of softwood trunks with the rounded cutting edge of the Egyptian adz. In connection with the roof construction of the tent buildings it should be noted that the fluted masts support on brackets the ribs of the arched roof; these brackets are missing from the posts in brick buildings, and here they take the form of lateral overhanging plant leaves. At the top of the masts are reproduced sawn-off branches in stylized form. The mortises probably served for the insertion of horns, like those on the old tent palaces of the nomad chieftains.

Most of the structures within the burial precinct are simply solid sham-buildings that have mere niches or short passageways for cult images or ritual processions. The only ones with interior rooms are the lengthy entrance hall, the "sacristy," and the living quarters of the king which are built onto the north side of the step pyramid. The disposition of the various buildings within the precinct and their interconnection by means of real passages or false doors did not have to correspond exactly with the residential prototype, but were determined by special requirements of the burial rite and the cult of the dead. For example, the triple-aisled hallway through which the funeral procession entered the sacred precinct had assumed the role of "palm grove of Buto"; thus the stone columns are decorated with a fringe of palm fronds.

This first stone-built mortuary complex, whose architectural organization and formal design already indicate a high level of accomplishment, has been identified from inscriptions as the work of the king's chief architect Imhotep, who simultaneously served as high priest of Heliopolis.

The Pyramid Complexes of the Fourth and Fifth Dynasties
The transition from the Third to the Fourth Dynasty was accompanied by a fundamental change in the planning and design of the royal tombs. The Lower Egyptian or Memphite concept of the tomb was abandoned; no longer was it a residence for the afterlife, nor the funerary precinct a realistic open-air stage setting for ritual performance. Probably under the influence of the myth of the death and resurrection of the god Osiris, the death of the king now became a mythical fate, whose "mysteries" permeated the burial ceremonies and cult practices and established the principal theme of the new royal romb architecture. Subsequently the cult area was organized in the form of a "processional stage" along an architecturally defined "sacred way" that began at the edge of the desert and ended in the tomb chamber; therefore the rites were performed and the utterances recited in a succession of rooms, passages, courts, gates, and pillars.

The impetus for change came from Abydos, in Upper Egypt; there the procession led from the temple of the cemetery god through the flat desert valley to the royal burial ground in the west. The Upper Egyptian character of the new trend is also expressed in the development and exaggeration of

151. Saqqara, mortuary precinct
of King Zoser, east side of building
for government of Lower Egypt:
papyrus stalks as half-column
supports. Third Dynasty, c. 2650
B.C.

XIII. Saqqara, walls of the
mortuary precinct of King Zoser.

XIV. *Saqqara, mortuary precinct of*
King Zoser; left, step pyramid.

152. Saqqara, mortuary precinct of King Zoser, Jubilee Court with re-erected chapel of Upper Egyptian tent-building type. Third Dynasty, c. 2650 B.C.

the king's tomb into a pyramid. King Zoser's step pyramid had a rectangular plan; the next phase, the square plan of the step pyramid at Medum, came with the accession of the Fourth Dynasty, and after that the increasing abstraction led to the crystalline geometry of the true pyramid. The step pyramid at Medum next took over—again evidence of its origin in the Upper Egyptian tumulus—an offering temple on the east side. This, however, was still a primitive affair, a modest flatroofed building with two parallel antechambers before a small court with two steles. From a "valley temple" at the edge of the desert a walled causeway led up to the pyramid precinct. In the arrangement of this royal burial area at Medum—valley temple, causeway, and offering temple—the future theme and plan of the Memphite pyramid complexes are first stated.

The new ideas about divine kingship and the burial rite were most fully realized in the pyramid complexes built during the Fourth Dynasty by Chephren and Cheops at Giza, where these ideas are manifest in the enormous masses and in the use of hard stones, granite and basalt, and alabaster as building materials. Chephren significantly enlarged the valley temple and roofed over the causeway; his offering temple at the foot of the pyramid was preceded by a huge "veneration temple" with a row of statuary shrines as the "sanctuary." An immediate impression of this architecture can now be gained only from the valley temple, a square building with smooth sloping exterior walls. The masonry consists of a core of local limestone faced on both sides with massive slabs of granite. Also of granite are the pillars inside, and the architraves and roof beams, all monoliths. The floors are paved with white alabaster slabs.

The funeral procession arrived from the east, from the Nile Valley, first landing on the west bank in front of the valley temple; it split into two groups and entered the narrow antechamber through two portals bordered only by bands of inscriptions; reunited, it passed through a central doorway into the inverted T-shaped hypostyle hall with its square granite pillars. Ranged around the walls were twenty-three statues of Chephren enthroned, which figured in the ceremonies of the "Opening of the mouth." The thin light that found its way through the slit windows in the roof was reflected from the bright alabaster floor. These early monumental interiors are otherwise unadorned, and they achieve their effect exclusively from the interrelated masses, the construction, and the color and durability of the materials. The procession left the valley temple through a narrow passage and ascended for nearly one-third of a mile the covered causeway to the pyramid temple.

The pyramid temple was also completely sealed off from the outside world and shielded from profane eyes by its smooth sloping walls. In its design the two parts stand out plainly, the outer temple and the veneration temple. The spaces of the outer temple occupy the hollow core of the otherwise solid mass of stone; they repeat the arrangement of the valley temple

156. Medum, offering temple and two steles on east side of step pyramid; remains of enclosure wall and upper portion of causeway. Third-Fourth Dynasty, c. 2600 B.C.

157. Medum, step pyramid, from east; in foreground, site of former valley temple and causeway. Third-Fourth Dynasty c. 2600 B.C.

except that here the constriction of a passageway separates thematically the crossbar from the stem of the T-shaped hall. A court surrounded by granite pillars introduces the veneration temple; there is evidence that the indentations in these pillars contained enthroned images of the king. Beyond and side by side are the five deep shrines that composed the sanctuary proper, directly behind the five bays of the western row of pillars. The offering place of the Abydos type with its two steles probably occupied the space between the rear wall of the veneration temple and the foot of the pyramid. The procession followed a narrow passageway leading from the northwest corner of the pillared court directly into the walled pyramid precinct—bypassing the sanctuary—and continued to the passage on the north side of the pyramid that ended in the tomb chamber.

Already under Chephren's predecessor Radedef, the sun cult of Heliopolis had begun to exert an influence on the dogma of divine kingship and life in the hereafter, and the arrangements of the tomb were correspondingly affected. The Lower Egyptian heritage began to assume greater importance. It the mortuary temple of Radedef's tomb complex, north of Giza near Abu Roash, a system of columns with plant motifs replaces the more abstract architecture of pillars. These religious influences are unequivocal in the tombs of the late Fourth Dynasty. The pyramid shape was sometimes abandoned in favor of the "house tomb" form as, for example, in the tomb of Queen Khent-kaw-s in the necropolis of Giza with its "palace" rising above niched walls.

With the advent of the Fifth Dynasty sun worship became the state religion. In the choice of their tombs these kings reverted to the classical pyramidal form and adapted the Memphite mortuary temple to the demands of the new cult. The founder of the dynasty, King Weserkaf, shifted the mortuary temple to the south side of his pyramid at Saqqara in order to include the entire path of the sun in a ritual performed within a pillared court. His successors returned to the traditional axial arrangement with the temple on the east side of the pyramid; the stern blankness of the temple exteriors was relaxed, however, and colonnades were introduced to open up the valley temple, and sometimes the veneration temple, to the outside world. Columns in the form of palm trees and bundles of papyrus and lotus stalks supported the roofs of the porticoes; these ultimately derive from the early reed architecture, in which bundled plants were used as structural supports, and in their stone form they stand for the sun god, the divine myths, and the burial practices of Buto. On the axis of the sanctuary, at the base of the pyramid, another cult edifice with a vaulted ceiling was introduced; its false door, a Lower Egyptian element, displaced the Upper Egyptian offering place with steles that had originated at Abydos.

The decoration of the interior gives "cosmic" significance to the chambers of the Fifth Dynasty temples. Ceilings are painted blue with

158. *Giza, pyramids, from east;*
right to left, Cheops, Chephren,
Mycerinus. Fourth Dynasty,
2550-2480 B.C.

159. *Giza, valley temple of Chephren's pyramid complex; passage leading from antechamber to T-shaped hypostyle hall. Fourth Dynasty, c. 2520 B.C.*

160. *Giza, plan of temples in Chephren's pyramid complex: above, veneration temple adjoining pyramid; below, valley temple (from Smith, 1958).*

golden stars to represent the night sky; floors of black basalt represent the dark earth from which sprout plants in the form of columns.

The creative development of monumental tomb architecture came to an end with the close of the Fifth Dynasty. The mortuary temples of the kings of the Sixth Dynasty adhere strictly to the established plan and return to the closed structure and abstract pillars of an earlier period.

This change in the architectural organization and design of the royal tomb complexes of the Old Kingdom is not to be understood as a "stylistic mutation." Each complex shows individual planning. Upper and Lower Egyptian influences are interwoven as principal themes; in the course of development the relationships among chambers, halls, and passages are dissolved and the elements reshuffled. The architectural historian must take these complexes "apart again at the joints" and explain them as changes in "thematic functions." These functions are recognizable in the Pyramid Texts that first appear on the walls of the passages and tomb chambers in the pyramids from the late Fifth Dynasty. In their arrangement, progressing from the entrance to the heart of the pyramid, they correspond to the successive features of the valley temple, causeway, and pyramid temple. Thus the architectural development of the pyramid complexes becomes a sublime manifestation of continually changing rites and eschatological beliefs, and in these one can discern the spiritual tensions of the epoch and the clashes of contending principles and forces.

Temples of the Old Kingdom
Of the Old Kingdom sanctuaries of the gods at Memphis, nothing has survived. The only sanctuary of that period still standing is the temple of Qasr el Sagha, north of the Faiyum. On the basis of its construction of massive limestone blocks it probably belongs to the Fourth Dynasty; its plan is scarcely distinguishable from that of the sanctuaries of the pyramid temples. The seven shrines of the gods once worshiped here stand side by side on a raised platform. Each shrine concealed a cult image behind doors that could be opened and closed, and is bordered by a molding and crowned by a concave cornice. The row of shrines opens on a narrow passage bounded on the other side by the thick front wall of the building. In the middle of this wall, opposite the large central shrine of the principal deity, is the entrance to the temple. Small rooms on the two short sides of the sanctuary probably served for storing ritual accessories. No inscription reveals the names of the gods to whom this temple was dedicated.

The Sun Sanctuaries
It is possible that in the Old Kingdom the national gods had their shrines in the imposing mortuary temples of the kings and were included in an established cult. The growing influence of the sun god has already been mentioned, and the sun sanctuaries closely connected with the royal tombs

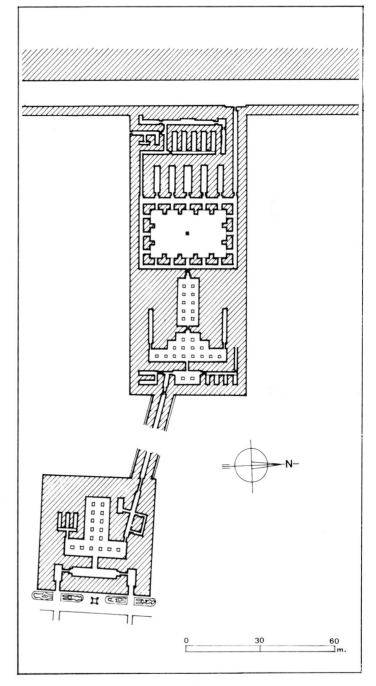

161. *Giza, valley temple of Chephren's pyramid complex; transversal area of T-shaped hypostyle hall.*

are, in the area of the capital, the only temples of which enough is preserved for a plausible reconstruction. For these temples, too, in which the day star was worshiped, there was no established architectural composition; it was determined by the evolving theological system of the sun cult.

Just north of Chephren's valley temple at Giza lie the remains of a monumental temple on the axis of the Great Sphinx immediately to the west. This temple of the Sphinx was dedicated to Harmakhis, or "Horus at the horizon," according to a New Kingdom inscription. The massive structure with sloping walls and concave cornices is accurately aligned with the four points of the compass. The outer and inner walls and the pillars of the inner court are faced with granite blocks, the smaller pillars and roof beams surrounding the court are granite monoliths. As in Chephren's valley temple, two entrances from the east lead into the building, emerging in the north and south pillared halls of the court, which is narrow and on a precise north-south axis. In front of the broad pillars surrounding the court extant remains indicate that seated figures of Chephren were placed there. The design of this unique building showed on the long east and west sides of the court a several-stepped niche, provided in each case with a row of six pillars and, nearer, a row of two. The ambulatories on the short north and south sides, in a modification of the original plan, were widened by another row of six pillars each.

The niche in the west wall is aligned with the Sphinx behind, which as "Horus at the horizon" equates the dead king with the evening sun; the eastern niche indicates due east, toward Horus reappearing as the morning sun. The twenty-four pillars in the four ambulatories constitute an allusion to the sun's daily journey. The two pairs of pillars in the niches probably represent the four pillars of the sky. The Harmakhis temple is therefore a monument and holy place of the sun god in the person of Horus, with whose disappearance in the evening the king was identified in the Sphinx and upon whose cyclical return every morning the king based his hopes of continued existence through eternity.

On the rim of the western desert, just north of their pyramids at Abusir, the kings of the Fifth Dynasty built sun sanctuaries of which two have so far been cleared. They were "monuments of the living king to his father Ra," and, after the death of their builders, probably served for the worship of that god, source of the perpetual renewal of both nature and the kingdom. As an architectural type, these temples constitute a special form that would seem to go back to the sanctuary of the sun god Ra in Heliopolis; the original model was probably a "primeval hill" with a monumental pillar, the benben stone. The first of these sanctuaries of the sun, built by the founder of the Fifth Dynasty, King Weserkaf, was made of brick; King Neuser-ra built his of limestone. It had an obelisk about 120 feet tall, constructed of white limestone blocks, and this stood on a sixty-foot-high granite-faced base with sloping walls on the west side of the court. The

XVI. *Giza, valley temple in Chephren's pyramid complex.*

162. *Giza, valley temple of Chephren's pyramid complex; longitudinal area of T-shaped hypostyle hall (statues of the king once stood against the walls).*

163. *Giza, pyramid of Chephren, Great Sphinx of Chephren, and pyramid of Cheops, from southeast.* ▷

164. *Giza, pyramid complex of Chephren: plan of Harmakhis temple, valley temple, and Sphinx (from Ricke, 1970).*

165. *Giza, Great Sphinx of Chephren and remains of Harmakhis temple, from east (behind, left and right: pyramids of Mycerinus and Chephren).*

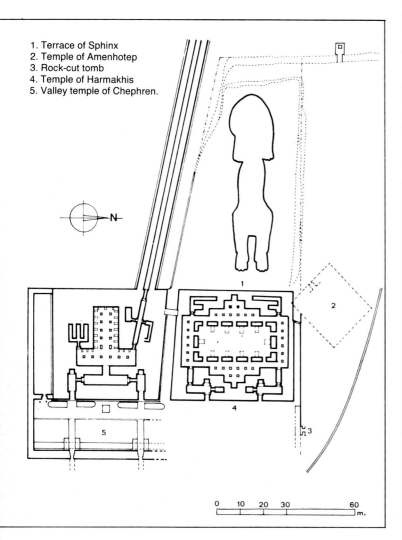

1. Terrace of Sphinx
2. Temple of Amenhotep
3. Rock-cut tomb
4. Temple of Harmakhis
5. Valley temple of Chephren.

N

0   10   20   30   60
m.

166. *Giza, pyramid complex of Chephren: Great Sphinx, from northeast.*

167. *Giza, "Buto type" tomb complex of Queen Khent-kaw-s. End of Fourth Dynasty, c. 2450 B.C.*

168. *Abusir, pyramid complex of Sahura, valley temple in foreground. Fifth Dynasty, c. 2440 B.C.*

169. *Abusir, reconstruction of sun sanctuary of Ne-user-ra. Fifth Dynasty, c. 2370 B.C. (from Smith, 1958).*

170. *Abusir, plan of pyramid complex of Sahura (from Smith, 1958).*

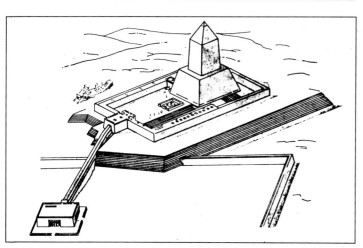

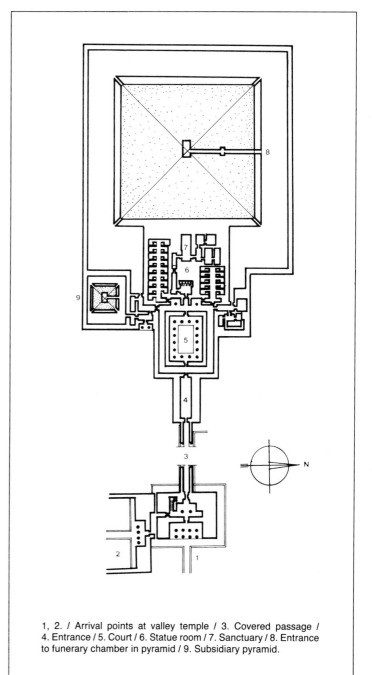

1, 2. / Arrival points at valley temple / 3. Covered passage / 4. Entrance / 5. Court / 6. Statue room / 7. Sanctuary / 8. Entrance to funerary chamber in pyramid / 9. Subsidiary pyramid.

171. *Aswan, west bank of Nile, tomb complexes, including causeways and double tomb of nomarchs Sabni and Mekhu. Sixth Dynasty, c. 2250 B.C.*

walled court was surrounded inside by a walled corridor. From the entrance on the east the portico ran along the south wall to the base of the obelisk, and from there interior ramps led to an upper platform in front of the east side of the base. In the court, in front of the obelisk base, open-air sacrifices were offered on a big altar built of massive alabaster blocks; north of the altar was an area where the sacrificial animals were slaughtered. Outside the sanctuary, to the south, are the brick foundations for a solar boat. The situation of the sun sanctuaries on the desert plateau made it necessary to build a valley temple with a causeway leading to the high ground, like those associated with the royal tombs.

The hieroglyphs for the names of the individual sun sanctuaries of the earlier Fifth Dynasty show only the base, whereas the later ones include an obelisk as well. In the Old Kingdom the obelisk is relatively thick in shape; in the Middle Kingdom and particularly in the beginning of the New Kingdom it became more slender and was made a feature of the architecture, generally paired in front of the pylons of the temple. It is derived from the Heliopolitan monumental pillar, the benben stone, the resting place of the sun. In the Old Kingdom, under the influence of the same abstracting tendencies that led to the true pyramid, it acquired the geometrical shape of a square tapering pillar with a pyramidal apex. Today of the Heliopolitan sanctuary only the sixty-five foot granite obelisk of Sesostris I still stands. However, we shall have occasion to mention Heliopolis again in connection with the planning of the temple of Amon-Ra at Karnak during the New Kingdom and, above all, the temple complexes at Amarna of the sun worshipper Akhenaten.

Tombs of the Royal Officials and Provincial Tombs
Just as the smaller graves of the courtiers were disposed around royal tombs in the cemeteries of the unifiers of Upper and Lower Egypt and their successors, at Memphis and Abydos, so in the later epochs the high state officials were buried near the tombs of their masters. In the Old Kingdom these dignitaries were typically buried in "mastabas," monumental tumulus tombs with sloping exterior walls, first built of brick but before long of squared limestone blocks. In the interior of this mass were first created—starting with the "door niche" as the offering place (false door)—narrow cult places, which were gradually widened into cult chambers; by the end of the development, in the tombs of the viziers of the Sixth Dynasty, these took over the entire core of the mastaba. During the Old Kingdom the offering place with the false door underwent many changes. The mastaba was also influenced by domestic architecture, as exemplified by the narrow pillared halls at the entrance or around the courts that preceded the tomb. Certain elements, such as the statuary shrines for the statue cult, were clearly borrowed from the royal tombs. In its spatial planning the mastaba has an evolution parallel to that of the royal mortuary temple during the Fifth and Sixth Dynasties; the plan was continually

being revised and adapted to conform to changes in the requirements of the cult.

Tomb-building practices outside the capital, in the nomes of Middle and Upper Egypt, had a decisive effect on the course of Egyptian monumental architecture. They were controlled by the local governors or nomarchs, a feudal nobility, who, starting as mere servants of the king, had become increasingly independent with the weakening of centralized power. In Middle and Upper Egypt the boundary between desert and fertile land is often marked by sharply rising ground; sometimes steep cliffs actually form the bank of the river, and the provincial tombs are mostly carved out of the living rock high up the cliff face. Their cult chambers and furnishings were patterned after the prototypes at the royal capital. The sequence of a forecourt in front of the rock-hewn tomb facade, a screened entrance hall supported by pillars, and a causeway was dictated by the physical nature of the site; in the provinces the burial arrangements may show many variations.

At Thebes, loose sediments form low hills between the rivers and the western cliffs. Here, as part of the tomb complexes of the local princes, huge courts could be excavated on a east-west axis: before the narrow west end of the court an open hall of stout pillars was carved out of the poor rock nearby; from the center aisle of this hall a level passage was tunneled westward to a cult chamber; the shaft went from here to the sarcophagus chamber. The retinue of the Theban prince was buried in separate graves in the side walls of the court.

THE MIDDLE KINGDOM

Neb-hepet-ra Mentuhotep's Mortuary Temple at Thebes (Deir el Bahari)

The collapse of the Old Kingdom was followed by a lengthy period of turmoil and internal disorder, during which no monumental buildings were erected. About 2050 B.C. Neb-hepet-ra Mentuhotep, a member of one of the princely houses of Thebes, succeeded in reuniting the Two Kingdoms. Thebes became temporarily the royal capital. On the east bank of the Nile, near the principal sanctuary from which later grew the temple complex of Karnak, lay the city with its palace, administrative buildings, and residential quarters. On the opposite (west) bank the dead had been buried since time immemorial at the foot of the impressive cliffs.

King Mentuhotep, founder of the Middle Kingdom, chose for his mortuary temple and burial place the edge of a valley leading into these western cliffs and ending in a sheer wall of solid rock (Deir el Bahari). This deep basin was probably already sacred to Hathor, goddess of the dead. Mentuhotep's mortuary temple is the first known monumental building in Upper Egypt and in Thebes. As a royal tomb and center for the worship of the king and the Theban gods, it had to give prominence to the new dynastic

order under the leadership of Thebes. The fabric of the temple has suffered severely from subsequent exploitation as a stone quarry and from rockslides. The design was strongly axial, leading from the edge of the fertile land to the tomb chamber of the king deep within the cliff. The facade faced east, toward the sanctuary of Karnak, where the cult of Amon can be traced back to the rise of Thebes. As in the royal mortuary complexes of Memphis, here too a valley temple (not preserved) gave access to a walled causeway that ascended to a broad walled court, terminating in the temple area abutting the western cliff. The final stretch of the approach to the temple was flanked by sycamores and tamarisks.

The temple itself stood on a raised terrace carved from the living rock; access from the court was by a massive central ramp. The base of the terrace was fronted with double porticoes on either side of this ramp. On the terrace was a broad freestanding building, square in plan, and upon it an elongated structure that extended west into the cliffside. The square structure had a massive core with sloping walls, pillared galleries ("ambulatories") on all four sides, and an outer ring of thick battered enclosing walls. Like the east face of the terrace, these walls were fronted by porticoes on east, north, and south. The openness of this architecture probably goes back to the earlier Theban princely tombs.

The western part of the temple was primarily dedicated to the worship of the dead ruler. Here was the entrance to the tomb chamber, in the floor of a small columned court that separated the "fore-temple" from the mortuary temple proper. The latter consisted of a wide hall, whose flat roof was supported by ten rows of eight columns, the oldest known hypostyle hall of any size in Egyptian architectural history. The holy of holies was a rock-cut chamber opening off the west side of this hall.

The design of the mortuary temple of King Mentuhotep is one of the most independent in Egyptian architecture. Since it was first discovered the assumption has been that the massive core structure at the east end of the terrace was once topped by a pyramid that rose above the flat roofs of the ambulatories and the outer walls, and this is the reconstruction found in all the histories of Egyptian art and architecture. Only recently, through the efforts of D. Arnold, has the underlying religious and lordly conception of the temple become apparent. According to Arnold, the core structure is a reflection of a primitive sanctuary excavated beneath the Monthu temple of Medamud (near Thebes), interpreted as the primeval abode of the deity Monthu-Ra worshipped in the Theban region and thus as a monumentalized "primeval hill." In the exercise of his authority on earth and in death the king had close ties with this local creator god. Mentuhotep's hypostyle hall carved out of the western cliff was devoted to the cult of the king, living and dead, and of the god Amon-Ra of Karnak; this is the first hint of the intimate relationship between the ruler and Amon-Ra that was to play so large a part in the New Kingdom mortuary temples at Thebes.

Beneath the core structure lies the dummy tomb of the king, reached

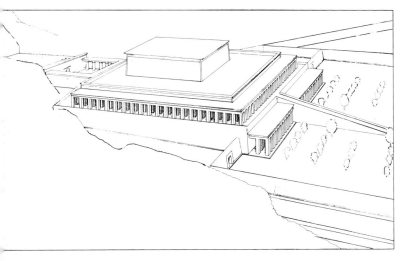

174. *Deir el Bahari (West Thebes), reconstruction of mortuary temple of Neb-hepet-ra Mentuhotep (from Arnold, unpublished).*

176. *Deir el Bahari (West Thebes), mortuary temple of Neb-hepet-ra Mentuhotep, from northwest.*

175. *West Thebes, tomb complex of Djar, broad court and pillared vestibule in manner of older princely tombs. Eleventh Dynasty, c. 2050 B.C.*

177. *Beni Hasan, cult chamber of rock tomb of Prince Kheti (detail). Eleventh Dynasty, c. 2000 B.C.*

178. *Beni Hasan, cult chamber of rock tomb of Prince Kheti. Eleventh Dynasty, c. 2000 B.C.*

179. *Aswan, west bank of Nile, rock tomb of Prince Sirenpowet II. Twelfth Dynasty, c. 1870 B.C.*

from the forecourt (Bab el Hosan), an Osiris tomb with which the plantings in the court were presumably related. The statues of the king in long festive robes, found in the broad temple courtyard, signify the earthly and eternal celebration of his royal jubilee and the perpetual rebirth of the ruler and the dynastic order that he embodied.

In Arnold's interpretation, which is consistent with the surviving fragments of the wall reliefs, Mentuhotep's mortuary temple was newly shaped by a theology and a conception of kingship that had developed from local Theban traditions. It was a unique creation representing influences that emerged in modified form in the terracing of the Twelfth Dynasty princely tombs of Qaw el Kebir and, some five hundred years later, in Hatshepsut's temple complex, its close neighbor to the north.

The Pyramid Complexes of the Twelfth Dynasty Kings

The kings of the Twelfth Dynasty also came from Thebes, but for political reasons they transferred their residence back to Memphis. At the same time they retained a particular affection for Thebes and adorned the nome with temples; after Memphis, Thebes became the most important religious center. South of Memphis, near Lisht and Dahshur, and farther south at Lahun and Hawara, on the edge of the Faiyum (an area that the kings of the late Twelfth Dynasty opened up for farming), lie the royal tombs built again in accordance with Memphite tradition, in the form of pyramids with mortuary temples. Only the tomb monument of Sesostris I near Lisht has enough architectural and sculptural remains to permit a plausible reconstruction. The plan of the mortuary temple is reminiscent of the pyramid complexes of the later Old Kingdom during the Sixth Dynasty. The pyramids of the Old Kingdom have neither the height nor the solidity of those built of squared stone blocks in the Old Kingdom. The position of kingship had changed, and confidence in the massiveness of tombs as a means of ensuring the continuance of eternal existence had been shaken by the political upheavals of the First Intermediate Period; also social changes had occurred that meant the labor resources of the entire country were no longer at the disposal of the Twelfth Dynasty kings.

Amenemhat I, founder of the Twelfth Dynasty, plundered the mortuary temples of Cheops and other kings of the Old Kingdom for granite blocks to build his own pyramid. All the pyramids of this period exhibit new techniques that are saving of both labor and materials. Their cores consisted either of sand and rubble, the mass held together by a radiating system of rubble walls, or entirely of sun-dried brick. Only the outer sides of the pyramids were carefully faced with white limestone slabs, and the apex was sometimes of dark granite. On the other hand, as compared with the Old Kingdom, greater resources were diverted toward safeguarding the royal tomb itself by the most solid possible construction for the sarcophagus chamber, sometimes hollowed from an immense monolith, and by blind corridors to defeat tomb robbers.

The most important of the mortuary temple complexes, that of Amenemhat III at Hawara, was known to the Greeks as the "labyrinth." Herodotus (*Histories*, II, 148) and Strabo (*Geography*, XVII, 1, 37) are among the ancient authors who have left descriptions of this enormous structure, of which almost nothing now remains. Attempts to reconstruct it exclusively on the basis of these accounts have been only partially successful.

Provincial Burials of the Twelfth Dynasty Nomarchs

Apart from its kings, the Twelfth Dynasty also had its feudal nobility, the princely families of Middle and Upper Egypt who constituted an influential and largely independent power. Near their provincial capitals on the gently or steeply sloping flanks of the hills that fringed the Nile Valley they also built rock tombs, some of which vied in lavishness, spaciousness, and independence of design with the mortuary complexes of the kings. Because of their excellent state of preservation they add greatly to our understanding of the tomb architecture of the period.

The rock tombs at Beni Hasan in Middle Egypt reflect the Lower Egyptian concept of the tomb as a representative eternal "abode" and "residence" of the dead. The rock chamber of one of the older tombs is furnished with papyrus-bundle columns, and represents a "festival hall" that may have existed–built of less permanent materials–in the palaces of the princes. The entrances often lie beneath an open porch of a kind also found in the contemporary houses of the nobility. In the later princely tombs at Beni Hasan a stricter emphasis on cult requirements and royal prototypes produced a deep, axially oriented, three-aisled rock chamber. The sections of ceiling between the longitudinal architraves are flat vaults, and rest on polygonal pillars; exactly opposite the entrance in the rear wall of the middle aisle stands a niche containing the statue of the owner of the tomb. The vaulted ceilings over the three aisles are painted with elements characteristic of the tentlike festival halls, colorful carpet patterns and simulated wooden ribs, whose perishable counterparts have not survived.

Upper Egyptian ideology, on the other hand, corresponds to the abstraction of architectural forms, and serves only the ceremonial fulfillment of the cult along a strong axially directed spatial sequence. The tomb of Prince Sirenpowet II on the west bank near Aswan is a grandiose example of the axial plan oriented strictly east and west. From the lofty three-aisled entrance hall, with its flat ceiling and square pillars, one continues westward over low steps that lead to a long passageway with a low-vaulted roof, ending in the cult chamber. The floor of this passageway sinks by imperceptible degrees to permit sunlight to pass through the tall entrance door into the cult chamber and fall on the richly painted sanctuary with the statue of the deceased. In their architectural plan and articulation, the most highly developed of the princely tombs are those at Qaw el Kebir (east bank, south of Assiut). From a broad columned forehall built of brick at the foot of the hill a covered causeway led up to the mortuary complexes; these are in many stories that overlap the slopes, and through open stairways the cliff spaces are linked with screened forecourts, pillared halls, and sanctuaries in wide hollowed-out halls. This is the articulation of the royal mortuary temple adapted to the exigencies of a hillside site. The resemblance, moreover, is not merely external; the thematic correspondence of the sequences of rooms and the furnishings with those of the royal tombs extends even to the details.

The Temples

From the Middle Kingdom there are more important remains of temples than from the Old Kingdom. They were frequently, even in the Twelfth Dynasty, still constructed of brick, and through later renovations in stone their remains, though widely scattered throughout the land, are scanty indeed and often insufficient to permit an intelligible reconstruction of the plans. Nonetheless, it is clear from the little that survives that the architecture of the Middle Kingdom put into effect certain new ideas that were to have a decisive influence on the future organization of the sanctuaries of the gods. One might mention the sanctuaries that now appeared for the first time in temples in the neighborhood of Thebes, at Medamud (northeast of Karnak) and Tod (south of Luxor): these had closing doors at front and rear and were approached through a broad hall of pillars or columns. They served, like later examples from the Eighteenth Dynasty, as permanent or temporary repositories for the images of the gods and their barges, and indicate that these images were carried in procession to other sanctuaries inside and outside their own temple. An unusual feature of the small temple built by Amenemhat III and IV on the edge of the Faiyum at Medinet Madi is the antechamber supported by two papyrus-bundle columns between side walls extended to the front to protect the entrance. Inside, the arrangement of the three shrines for the statues of the gods honors a tradition going back to the time of the pyramids.

The two-towered "pylon," so characteristic of the monumental entrances of the walled temples after the beginning of the New Kingdom, has its origins in the Middle Kingdom, as excavations at Hermopolis have shown. The pylon towers were probably the end result of a process of thickening and raising the front walls of large courts on either side of a lower entrance gate. The gate towers ("pylons") have battered walls on all sides, beaded fillets at the corners, and an encircling concave cornice at the top. In the front walls are narrow recesses, varying in number, and on holidays these contained tall masts with colorful pennants. The masts were steadied by wooden braces projecting from narrow window openings high above the recesses. Inside the pylons stairs led to the upper rooms and the flat roof. Between the two gate towers was sandwiched the lower main portal of the temple, also crowned with a concave cornice. In late texts the

pylons are designated as the "hills of the horizon," between which the sun rises. The late identification of the two gate towers with the goddesses Isis and Nephthys probably derives from the mythological concept that these two goddesses bear up the rising sun in their arms.

The pylons give the temple facade and its entrance portal a strong accent and unique monumentality. At the same time, their fortress-like aspect clearly expresses the idea of the defense of the temple entrance against all hostile powers. Accordingly, from the Nineteenth Dynasty on, the kings recorded their victorious battles, or the god's bestowal of a victory-promising weapon, on the outer walls of the pylons. Against the two narrow sides or the rear of the pylons abutted the walls that enclosed the temple. In the New Kingdom paired obelisks were often erected in front of the pylons, one on either side of the temple entrance. A single obelisk, originally symbolizing the resting place of the sun god, was first erected of limestone blocks in the Fifth Dynasty sun sanctuaries. Since the Old Kingdom the center for the worship of the sun god Ra had been the sanctuary at Heliopolis, the site of the "primeval hill" with the benben stone, which had established the pattern for the Old Kingdom sanctuaries of the sun. At the beginning of the Twelfth Dynasty Sesostris I had a rectangular temple built over the low roundish sacred primeval hill of Heliopolis. Of this building one of the two sixty-five-foot rose-granite monolithic obelisks that once flanked the main entrance is all that still stands. This pair of obelisks also suggests an entrance portal between gate towers, of which, however, nothing at Heliopolis has survived. Excavations there have merely established the east-west orientation of the temple and an avenue of sphinxes that led from the bank of the Nile to the main gate. A few clues to the former appearance of Heliopolis, this important sanctuary and theological center, are supplied by the fragments of a stone tablet of the seventh century B.C., now in the Museo Egizio in Turin, bearing traces of an incised temple plan. The reconstruction shows an axial succession of three courts, each entered through a portal between gate towers. Tall flagpoles rise above the pylons of the first court, while those of the third court may have been preceded by a pair of obelisks. In the second court pillared galleries are indicated along the side walls; an adjacent sanctuary on the right has been included in the court for lack of space at the right edge of the tablet. In the third court a transverse row of pillars cuts off a narrower area in the front where, against the side wall on the right, a mighty altar is built, reached by two short flights of steps.

Open courts entered through a portal between gate towers are also characteristic of the temple of Karnak, dedicated to Amon-Ra, whose expansion dates from the beginning of the New Kingdom. This is particularly true of the core of the sanctuary, which Tuthmosis I enclosed with walls, and of the south axis of the temple developed by his successors. An altar in an open court for the worship of the Heliopolitan sun god Ra-Harakhte has been preserved on the north side of the upper terrace of Queen Hatshep-

sut's temple at Deir el Bahari; there was another at Karnak. The sanctuary of Heliopolis was most faithfully copied under Amenhotep IV (Akhenaten), introducer of the exclusive cult of the day star (Aten), in the Aten sanctuary at Karnak and, above all, in the Aten temples of the new capital Akhetaten (Tell el Amarna).

An early Twelfth Dynasty sanctuary, richly adorned with delicate reliefs, was dismantled into blocks and used as fill in the building of the third pylon of the temple of Karnak. The parts have since been fully reconstructed; it is the "White Chapel" of Sesostris I, which the king built on the occasion of his jubilee for Amon of Thebes and Min of Coptos, the fertility god assimilated by Amon. This almost square pavilion stands on a low podium accessible at either end by ramps between low stairsteps. The building rests on four angle pillars with round fillets at the outer corners, and on two intermediate pillars on each side; these support architraves and a flat roof crowned with a concave cornice. Between the pillars the spaces, except for the two entranceways, are bridged by low parapets rounded on top. Inside, a small rectangular space is formed by four pillars, and in the center is a granite pedestal on which stood an image of the king or the god. The "white Chapel" may be regarded as the oldest surviving example of a "baldachin temple," representing in stone and in monumentalized forms the ancient shrine beneath an awning.

The Middle Kingdom also shows the first appearance of "Osiris statues" in an architectural context. In these the ruler is portrayed in a standing position, entirely swathed in a close-fitting garment that even covers the feet and leaves only the hands free to clasp the scepters in a crossed position over the breast; Osiris, the god of death, is similarly portrayed in his cult images and other representations. At the mortuary temple of Sesostris I at Lisht such approximately lifesize statues flanked the probably unroofed approach to the temple, and thus they represented the king, with the crown of Upper or Lower Egypt on his head, as Osiris "risen." A colossal statue of the same king and the same type stood within the temple precinct of the god Osiris at Abydos; it was probably propped against a pillar and belonged as architectural sculpture to an open court of that temple. In the New Kingdom, after the beginning of the Eighteenth Dynasty statues on the same colossal scale appeared in front of interior walls, or before pillars of open halls around the wider courts, to provide architectural accents as well as to illustrate the functions of the building. They relate to the jubilee festival that the king usually celebrated at the end of the thirtieth year of his reign—that is, as an aging ruler. In these ceremonies were renewed the king's powers over the stage of a ritual death as Osiris, to permit his rebirth as Horus.

The architecture of the Middle Kingdom contributed many new forms to the design of sanctuaries, despite the paucity of its remains, and these the much more important architecture of the New Kingdom was quite willing to exploit.

INTERIOR SPACES AND SUPPORTS

Egyptian stone architecture began with imitative building forms, with three-dimensional representations of constructed types developed to serve the royal cult of the dead at the time of the first unification of Upper and Lower Egyptian traditions. The dummy buildings of King Zoser's mortuary precinct, translations into stone of tents and structures of matting and brick that were furnishings of the Memphis residence for use in the afterlife, can be converted back into the original building method according to their construction features. In Zoser's capital tent and matting buildings had already been translated into more durable brick while preserving their typical outward appearance. The "sacristy" in the king's mortuary precinct, as an imitation brick building with interior spaces, shows the characteristic spatial division of a brick house: the rooms are narrow, based on the spans and carrying capacity of the palm trunks which formed the flat roof. Posts are used sparingly.

In granite block construction the mortuary temple complexes of the pyramids had, since Cheops, been characterized by roofed multi-aisled halls from which opened courts and antechambers, whose flat stone ceilings were supported on square pillars. The monumental halls, passages, and courts were intended for rites celebrated at "way stations" on a processional route within the massive walls of the valley and pyramid temples. This arrangement of wide spaces articulated by rows of pillars, is far removed from the old idea of a "residence." Granite block construction imposes its own imperatives of building statics and mathematics. But what origin has this conception of space?

Obviously, it was the system of supports of the tent palace, monumentally reproduced in brick and wood, that the first prompted the unlimited increase of piers supporting the roof to create broad spaces in stone construction. The flat roofs of the stone buildings go back to the typical system of the brick house, palm trunks laid across architraves supported on wood posts.

Flat terrace roofs are characteristic of Egyptian monumental architecture, from the Old Kingdom to the buildings of the last Pharaohs. The roofs were reached by stairs from the inside of the building and were also often involved in the cult ritual. This type of roof, screened from view by continuing the exterior walls upward to form a parapet, was made possible by the minimal rainfall of the climate, even in the north of the country, but some provision had still to be made for drainage. The roof was given a slight pitch to deflect water from the occasional rainstorms into a system of gutters and outlets in the parapet walls; from the Fifth Dynasty until the end of the Late Period the waterspouts took the form of the foreparts of a lion. These lions were supported on regularly spaced blocks projecting far out from the face of the wall at roof level and the water flowed from between their outstretched paws. As an integral part of architectural sculpture,

182. Karnak, "White Chapel"
of Sesostris I. Twelfth Dynasty,
c. 1950 B.C.

these Egyptian lions are the equivalent of the lion-head waterspouts on Greek temples—probably borrowed from Egypt. The Egyptians saw a close connection between the lion, as lord of the desert, and the storms that blew in from the desert to strike the Nile Valley, and it also represented an apotropaic power, warding off evil from these indispensable openings in the temple walls.

In the Old Kingdom the pillar occurs in its original abstract square form without base or bearing slab (abacus). Not until the early Middle Kingdom were the edges shaved off to make it an eight- or sixteen-sided shaft, standing on a flat round base and supporting the architrave on an abacus. Thus the polygonal pillar is an approximation of the column form. Eventually the narrow vertical faces of the sixteen-sided pillar were fluted, thus continuing the tradition of the fluted supports in King Zoser's tent- and brick-style buildings, traceable to wood prototypes.

Occasionally in the Fourth Dynasty and more commonly in the Fifth, "plant columns" of various kinds began to be used in stone architecture for the support of beams. Within the royal mortuary temples they not only took over the functions of the abstract pillar but had their own thematic significance in the architectural scheme, now modified by the new solar religion; they also had their particular message recalling the prototypes in Egyptian mythology.

The idea of using bundled plant stems as supports goes back to prehistoric construction of light mat-buildings, a technique by which herdsmen and birdcatchers build their huts even in historic times.

Plant columns came to be the most usual type of support in Egyptian monumental architecture, and not only in sacred buildings of stone but also in houses and palaces, where, with no mythological reference, they are cut from wood and stand on stone bases, supporting wooden ceiling beams. Finally, plant forms must also be the the origin of the fluted masts in the facade of the stone reproduction of a tent building in Zoser's mortuary precinct, and certainly of the leaflike form at the top on either side of the roof rib. Apotropaic horns were inserted in the fronts of these masts. The two round bosses near the top of the masts, to be interpreted as stylized sawn-off branches, show that the memory was still fresh of the plant stems of the prehistoric tent structures, and of their translation into pine poles in the monumental royal tent.

The three-sided papyrus-topped stalks with open bell-shaped flowers, that represent supports in the facade of the building branching off the tent hall at right angles, may likewise have originated in wood construction. They are symbolical in character. In stone construction, as plant columns without a plinth, they represent the heraldic plant of Lower Egypt, comparable in this function to the granite heraldic pillars in Tuthmosis III's "hall of annals" in the temple of Karnak, the northern pillar decorated with three papyrus stems in painted high relief, while the southern one bears the lily-like plant of Upper Egypt.

Columns in the shape of an individual papyrus plant, with rounded shaft and an open bloom for the capital, appear for the first time in the Eighteenth Dynasty under Amenhotep III in the long entrance hall of the temple of Luxor. Like all Egyptian plant columns they carry the heavy architrave on an abacus, but in the case of the papyrus column with an overhanging bell-shaped flower capital, and similarly in the palm-tree column, the abacus is so small in proportion that it almost disappears behind the spread of the capital. The free growing plant with its mythological connotations determined the form, not its supporting function within the structure.

The palm column does not actually represent the tree; around the top of the circular, only slightly tapering shaft are bound eight palm fronds. The turns of the binding, with the loop end hanging down, are unmistakably reproduced. The tips of the individual fronds are rounded and curve gently outward. The abacus, so small that it cannot be seen from below, nestles in the center of the cluster of fronds. The palm column, too, stands on a flat round base. The form unites several different ideas in its meaning. In early representations palms surrounding a designated place indicate the buildings of the Lower Egyptian prehistoric royal cemetery at Buto. In ancient times stakes driven into the desert soil, and probably bound around with palm fronds, represent the holy place as the setting for burial ceremonies in front of royal Memphite tumuli. The palm, however, is also the seat of the sun god, and in the mortuary temples of the Fifth Dynasty it alludes directly to the mythical relationship between the tree and the god. It was also reserved as a heraldic plant of Upper Egypt, and for this reason palm columns were used in the royal palaces and in temple chambers set apart for the royal cult.

The lotus column likewise makes its first appearance in stone form during the Fifth Dynasty. It represents the stylization of a bundle of six lotus stalks that spring without swelling or shrinking from the round base to the flower capital, beneath which they are tied together. Six buds, only slightly open, stretch steeply upward to form the capital, on which rests a sturdy-looking abacus. Six small stalks with opening buds are inserted into the binding between the main stalks. In the realm of myth the lotus, too, was closely related to the sun god, who emerged from the primeval flood on a lotus blossom and rejoiced in its fragrance.

The papyrus-bundle column occurs much more frequently, and is related in form to the lotus column. Its first examples in monumental stone are also in the Fifth Dynasty. Eight three-sided stalks swell from their sheaths at the base of the column and taper up to the bands beneath the capital, consisting of eight closed buds that support the abacus as in the lotus column. Here, too, smaller stalks are tucked into the binding between the main stalks. From early times until the Eighteenth Dynasty each papyrus stalk was modeled to display its triangular front edge; under the Ramessids the column shaft was unified by suppressing the stalks.

Papyrus-bundle columns in the halls of the temples represent, according to a late temple inscription, the primeval landscape of the Nile Valley, "a papyrus thicket" in which the god walked. As elements of the world created by the gods, all the plant columns belong to the "cosmic" theme of the temple. They sprout from their low round bases like plants from the "primeval hill"; above them spreads the flat roof painted with golden stars on a dark blue ground to represent the night sky. Plant designs on the lower strips of the temple walls complete the meaning of the temple as an untouched divine creation where the gods could be thought to dwell. Likewise the closed bud capitals of the lotus and papyrus columns may symbolize the night, from which the temple and its inhabiting god are aroused in the morning rites.

A column of a special sort is the Hathor column, of Middle Kingdom origin. It was restricted to sanctuaries of the goddess Hathor and goddesses associated with her, and represents the goddess' rod-shaped fetish which was also carried in procession on festival occasions. The round shaft bears as its capital the masklike face of the goddess, her long hair framing her features and the lower ends curling behind her bovine ears; on her head she bears the "sistrum," a musical rattle that was sounded in her worship. The face of Hathor with its sistrum crown often decorates both front and back of the capital or even all four sides.

The stone "tent pole" column is known only from the great festival hall of Tuthmosis III in the temple of Karnak. In it are copied the slim wooden poles that supported the canopy over the royal throne, translated into stone forms. Tuthmosis III, to mark his jubilee, set up columns of this type in a court surrounded by pillared galleries to transform the area into a tentlike festival hall.

To these supports should be added the eight- and sixteen-sided "pillars" which, having a flat base and abacus, are also classed as columns.

Starting with the Amarna period the classical forms of the plant column, above all the palm column, underwent substantial changes, particularly in relation to the capitals; this arose from their use as supports in the official reception halls and audience chambers of the royal palaces. (Since these columns were made of wood, they survive only in fragmentary form). From these models come the numerous forms of the "composite capital" in the stone temples of the Late Period.

Because the tomb was regarded as the "abode" of the deceased, and the temple as the "castle," "palace," or dwelling of the god, the succession and design of spaces and the architectural construction of the royal palaces and the residences of the nobility exerted influence over the monumental sacred architecture. Open porticoes and halls articulated with rows of supports, as in the rock tombs of Beni Hasan, furnish decisive evidence about royal palaces and noble houses. As originally conceived, these were most probably derived from the arrangement and construction of the tent palace, transformed in the course of a long period of settled existence into

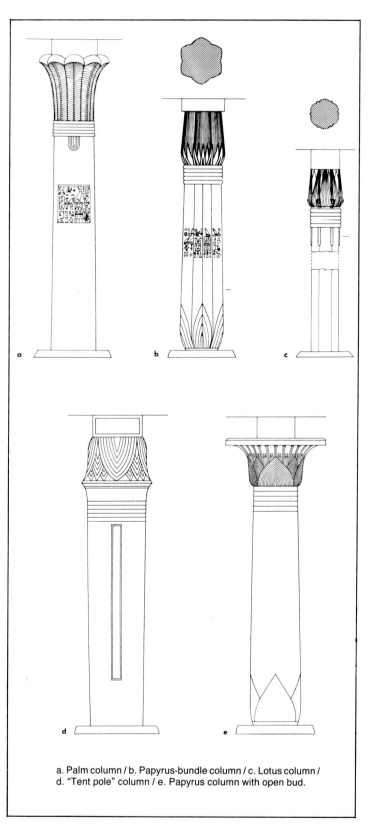

a. Palm column / b. Papyrus-bundle column / c. Lotus column / d. "Tent pole" column / e. Papyrus column with open bud.

structures of sun-dried brick with timber roof and posts. From the earliest times to the end of pharaonic civilization. Nile-mud bricks and wood were regarded as the prime building materials for residential construction, being well suited to the hot Egyptian climate. The brick walls and earthen floors were plastered over and painted. The ceilings, supported on wooden columns, consisted of beams of imported pinewood over which matting was stretched, then plastered and painted. The wooden columns were also gaily painted, and stood on flat stone bases. The sills and frames of the main doorways, which had to carry the weight of the wooden doors, were made of limestone blocks. On the uprights were bands of inscriptions, and on the broad lintels were inscriptions and figured compositions; inlays of glass paste and faience were sometimes used instead of painted relief.

The foundations of settlements with the modest dwellings of Old Kingdom artisans and laborers are now preserved near the Giza necropolis. At Lahun, on the edge of the Faiyum, the remains of an entire town, built on a unified plan, have been cleared; its buildings housed the workers and superintending officials employed at the nearby site of the pyramid of Sesostris II. A palace, now almost vanished, was built on high ground north of the town, apparently for the occasional use of the king. The town is entirely surrounded by thick walls and divided internally into several rectangular quarters by other walls. The streets are parallel and straight. Within each quarter the houses, compressed together cheek by jowl, are identical in size and spatial division. The spacious premises of the officials are ranged along the north wall of the town. Within each estate is a complicated arrangement of corridors and connecting rooms between the quarters for women and servants, kitchens and pantries, that always surround the inner courts; the typical suite occupied by the master of the house can be readily distinguished by its clearly discernible plan. The apartment faces north and consists first of a patio on whose south side stood a portico open to the cool north wind; through the portico is a broad antechamber leading to the central hall, a reception room whose ceiling rests on four columns. Beyond is the small private living room, as well as bedroom and bath. This suite is the core of the official house, and the same clear scheme is found in the royal palaces of Amarna, large and small, and in the houses of the officials.

Great triple-aisled columned halls with a dais for the throne that faced the entrance in the opposite wall, and wide columned halls that formed entry rooms to smaller audience chambers, are clearly recognizable in the plan of Amenhotep III's palace at Malkata, west of Thebes. Along either side of the great central columned hall were the suites for the ladies of the royal harem, also divided into a small antechamber, a throne room, and a connecting bedroom and bath.

At the end of the Eighteenth Dynasty the royal capital was transferred to the east Delta; Thebes remained only as the center of worship of the god

119

184. *Deir el Bahari (West Thebes), funerary temple of Queen Hatshepsut, from east. Eighteenth Dynasty, c. 1480 B.C.*

Amon-Ra and the burial place of the kings. Accordingly small palaces, apparently occupied only briefly by the ruler during the great festivals, were annexed to the royal mortuary temples on the west bank. These were always built against the south wall of the first court, and were connected with it by the "window of appearances." The best preserved palace of this kind is that of Ramesses III at Medinet Habu. Immediately adjacent to the wall of the temple court room containing two columns, and steps which lead up to the "window of appearances." From here the king participated in the solemn ceremonies performed in the first court, and received and rewarded deserving officials. The main room of the palace is the great hall, divided into three aisles by six columns, with a dais on which stood the king's throne and beyond it a smaller throne room for more intimate receptions. Smaller suites on the south of the main temple, from which they are separated by a corridor, each contain a bedroom and bath for the king and his retinue.

The roofs of the palace retain clear marks of their original form, where they were added to the stone outer wall of the first temple court. The reception rooms had longitudinal vaults resting on architraves supported by palm columns. The central block containing the royal halls was considerably taller than the apartments on either side and was lit by small stone-grilled windows in the clerestory.

In the permanent residences, which also included government buildings, temples, and quarters for the officials—for example, in the palace complexes of Amenhotep III in West Thebes and Amenhotep IV (Akhenaten) in Amarna—all the arrangements and especially the royal rooms were much more spacious. In both instances the painted decoration that filled the rooms has been preserved. The floor painting stretches from portal to portal representing the "royal way," decorated with bound and prostrate figures of Egypt's neighbors. Other floor paintings represent the primeval Egyptian landscape with swampy thickets where calves scramble and birds flutter overhead, thus hinting at the king's mythical role as "god of creation" and guarantor of world order, as well as his duty to beat off and destroy the nation's enemies.

THE NEW KINGDOM

Following the collapse of order at the end of the Middle Kingdom the "Hyksos," mercenary leaders from the Near East, established themselves in the east Delta and gradually extended their rule to Memphis and Middle Egypt. Upper Egypt remained virtually untouched by the invaders. It was again the princes of Thebes who had to expel the foreigners and found a new united kingdom, thus preparing the way for the most brilliant era of Egyptian civilization. By pursuing the Hyksos into their Palestinian homeland, and by other conquests in the north and in the south, deep into

185. *Deir el Bahari (West Thebes),
funerary temple of Queen
Hatshepsut, first terrace: right,
entrance hall to Anubis chapel; left,
north portico of facade ("birth
room"). Eighteenth Dynasty,
c. 1480 B.C.*

the Sudan, there arose a powerful Egyptian empire that lasted, with
Thebes as its capital and religious center, for two hundred years.

One of the prerequisites of this renaissance was a renewal of the conception of kingship. According to the new official dogma the legitimate ruler
was begotten by the god Amon-Ra and the sister-consort, now exalted to
"consort of the god," of the ruling king. In death the ruler entered into the
being of his divine father Amon.

At the beginning of the New Kingdom Thebes was still a young city
whose historical traditions did not extend beyond the local nomarchs, from
whom Neb-hepet-ra Mentuhotep, founder of the Middle Kingdom, had
stemmed. The new capital had to establish its visible supremacy through
the superiority of its system of gods and a display of monumental sanctuaries. In the Middle Kingdom Thebes had become the adode of Amon,
the creator god, who, by appropriating nearby cults such as that of the
primeval fertility god Min of Coptos and finally the sun god Ra of
Heliopolis, had developed into a univerasal divinity and "king of the
gods." The military victories had been won in Amon's name and into his
sanctuaries streamed most of the booty, and the tributes of the conquered
peoples. Amon-Ra became the national deity. He acquired the Theban
goddess Mut as his consort and the moon god Khonsu as their son. From
now on this family of gods formed a triad, with coordinated sanctuaries at
Karnak. Each member of the triad possessed near his cult image a sacred
barge, and in these the images could be taken to visit one another within
Thebes.

Apart from these principal Theban gods, the cults of other important
deities, such as Ptah of Memphis, had already found their way to Thebes
during the Middle Kingdom; these sanctuaries were also expanded under
the New Kingdom rulers.

The active construction of temples for the gods and of royal mortuary
temples began immediately under the first kings of the Eighteenth Dynasty, and it aimed at giving monumental expression to the various theological
systems newly drawn together; their arrangement turned the entire area of
Thebes into "Amon's city."

The district of the capital city of Thebes extended along both banks of
the Nile. On the east bank stood the royal palaces, with the government
buildings and residential quarters between the boundaries of the principal
sanctuary of Karnak on the north and the sanctuary of Luxor on the south,
both dating from the Middle Kingdom. On the edge of the west bank, confined by its cliffs, lay the necropolis, which had as its first monumental
center the tomb complex of the founder of the Middle Kingdom in the
valley at Deir el Bahari. Here lie buried also the kings of the New Kingdom,
but for reasons of security the royal tombs were tunneled into the rock in
the lonely Valley of the Kings in the western hills, physically separated
from the temples for the worship of the dead. The royal mortuary temples
were ranged at the foot of the cliffs that run in a line north and south, facing

186, 187. Deir el Bahari (West Thebes), funerary temple of Queen Gatshepsut, first terrace: left, "birth room," center, Anubis chapel; right, north colonnade. Eighteenth Dynasty, c. 1480 B.C.

XVII. *Deir el Bahari (West Thebes), funerary temple of Queen Hatshepsut.*

XVIII. *Medinet Habu, temple of Ramesses III, colossus statues of the main courtyard.*

188. Deir el Bahari (West Thebes), funerary temple of Queen Hatshepsut, south end of first terrace: Hathor chapel, interior of rock-cut sanctuary. Eighteenth Dynasty, c. 1480 B.C.

the fertile land and the sanctuaries on the east bank: they were memorial temples in the true sense of the word, serving not only for the cult of the king and his followers but also for the worship of Amon-Ra and other gods. Also on the west bank, further to the south and beyond the limits of the original city there has been found a "primeval hill" that was probably already extant in the Middle Kingdom.

The sanctuaries of the gods of Thebes were certainly independent buildings that were erected for specific reasons and especially in connection with jubilee festivals as "memorials of the kings for their father Amon," but their planning played an important role for the neighboring cults.

The Temple of Amon-Ra at Karnak

The remains of the oldest sanctuary of Karnak, rebuilt in the Twelfth Dynasty, are so scanty that the ground plan can no longer be established with certainty. It formed the core of all later expansions. Its east-west orientation was determined by the Nile from which a canal probably led to the forecourt of the temple at an early date. Because the temple was expanded continually toward the west the landing place, with its small obelisks and an avenue of ram-sphinxes leading to the later main entrance of the sanctuary, was likewise shifted westward, and its existing remains date only from late in the New Kingdom.

The history of the sanctuary is complicated by repeated expansions and by razing old shrines and constructing new ones, in the principal east-west directions and toward neighboring cults on north and south, a process that lasted from the beginning of the New Kingdom into the Late Period. Only traces are left of many of the buildings. Accordingly we can only discuss the basic conception of the architectural layout with reference to the more important elements of the temple, and describe the most notable sites.

So many cults gathered around the main temple of Amon-Ra, the king of the gods, that Karnak had the name "Collector of Holy Places." The decisive influence on planning during the Eighteenth Dynasty was Amon's taking over of the essence of the sun god. The connection with the Heliopolitan place of worship of Ra, with its pylons, obelisks, and wide courts, was thus supplied by the essence of the national deity. King Tuthmosis I was responsible for a considerable widening of the boundaries of the Middle Kingdom sanctuary, which he enclosed with stone walls on north, south, and east; on the west, toward the Nile, he built two monumental portals in close succession, between gate towers. Inside the giant court, against the enclosure walls, he set up statues in the form of Osiris, symbolizing the perpetual renewal of the kingship within the dynastic order: here began the furnishing of buildings with sculptures closely associated with the architecture. On either side of the gateway in the broader and taller front pylon (present pylon IV) Tuthmosis I erected sixty-five-foot obelisks of rose granite, of which the southern one still

189. *Deir el Bahari (West Thebes), funerary temple of Queen Hatshepsut, north wall of second terrace: interior of chapel of Tuthmosis I. Eighteenth Dynasty, c. 1480 B.C.*

190. *Medinet Habu (West Thebes), reconstruction of Queen Hatshepsut's baldachin temple, in original state (from Holscher, 1933).*

191. *Medinet Habu (West Thebes), section and plan of Queen Hatshepsut's baldachin temple (from Borchardt, 1938).*

192. *Medinet Habu (West Thebes), remains of Queen Hatshepsut's baldachin chapel, from south. Eighteenth Dynasty, c. 1470 B.C.*

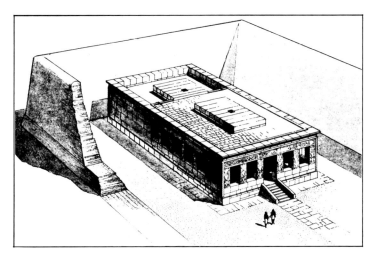

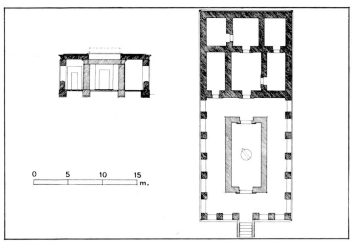

0   5   10   15
m.

stands. Between the two pylons (IV and V) was inserted a splendid hall with papyrus bundle columns and colossal standing figures of the king. The central precinct of the temple was thus permanently fixed. Here, within the zone of the Middle Kingdom sanctuary, Queen Hatshepsut built a red quartzite chamber for the processional barge and the cult image of the national god. Open to east and west, it was flanked by subsidiary chambers for religious implements. In the narrow court intervening between her father's pylons (IV and V) the queen raised two obelisks almost one hundred feet high, of which the northern one still stands.

At the same time she took in hand the south axis, that led from the forecourt in front of pylon IV to the temple of Mut and thence to the sanctuary of Luxor, and built pylon VIII, placing before it enthroned statues of colossal size. Her successor, Tuthmosis III, replaced the queen's red quartzite shrine with a new one in rose granite and in front of it he erected a small pylon (VI) as the entrance to his "hall of annals"; the ceiling rested on two slender square pillars decorated in painted high relief with the heraldic plants of Lower and Upper Egypt, the papyrus on the north pillar and the so-called lily on the south. In the hall of annals the conqueror recorded the details of his victorious campaigns against Palestine and Syria. Finally, Tuthmosis III erected two larger obelisks in front of the pair built by Tuthmosis I, but these have not survived.

The area enclosed by Tuthmosis I was extendend to the east by Tuthmosis III when he added a self-contained temple whose principal element was the great "festival hall" for the celebration of the king's jubilee. It consists of a court laid out at right angles to the main axis of the temple and ringed beyond by entrance halls supported on square pillars. In the middle of the eastern wall of the hall of columns lies the entrance to the holy of holies, which extends toward the east. Into this hall the king introduced two rows of tall columns, bearing a flat roof that is higher than the roofs of the surrounding halls; between the necessary supports the zone remained open, so that the interior suggests in cross section the appearance of a "basilica" with a clerestory. The orientation of the building, the mode of construction, and the form of the columns lining the central aisle, which resemble stone "tent poles," reveal that here two elements, a court with a festival tent erected in it, have been skillfully combined. Against the outside of the east wall of this jubilee hall the king built a small sanctuary facing east, and in front of it he erected a huge single obelisk, now standing before the Lateran Palace in Rome.

Tuthmosis III also developed the south axis of the temple, adding another pylon (VII) with colossal statues of the king on the south side. On the east side of the court formed between pylons VII and VIII he erected a small repository chapel that also leads to the "sacred lake" of the Karnak area. Sacred lakes were permanent features of Egyptian temples. They were the source of the holy water used in the ritual and, on festival occasions, the scene of excursions of the sacred barge. Along the banks there

were also enclosures with birds flying about in them, later to be used in ritual sacrifice. The pylons further along the south axis (IX and X) were built at the end of the Eighteenth Dynasty, pylon X serving also as the monumental southern entrance to the temple precinct. An avenue of sphinxes led south from here to the nearby temple of the goddess Mut, partially surrounded by its own horseshoe-shaped sacred lake.

The main temple was also enlarged westward, in the direction of the Nile, by the addition of further pylons. Sety I began the building of the great hypostyle hall at Karnak, in the courtyard between the pylons of Amenhotep III (III) and of Ramesses I (II); the enormous structure was completed by Ramesses II. It is of particular historical interest as the first true example of a building of the "basilica" type, that is, a long multi-aisled hall with a tall central aisle and much lower side aisles. The central aisle supports a ceiling on two rows of papyrus columns nearly eighty feet high with open bell-shaped blossoms as capitals. The two lower side areas containing the aisles have each sixty-one close-set papyrus-bundle columns forty feet high, of the smooth unified type introduced in the age of the Ramessides. The important clerestory zone between the roofs of nave and aisles consists of the supporting pillars and stone grilles between, which could have only dimly lighted the central aisle. The bands of inscriptions on the wall surfaces of this hall indicate that it served not as a real place of worship but as an assembly place for the sacred barges of the Theban triad at the time of processions. The barges were brought there from their sanctuaries "when Amon appeared at the festival to behold the beauty of the Theban region." Other "basilican" structures of this type, though on a much smaller scale, are found in the mortuary temple of Ramesses II (Ramesseum) on the west bank at Thebes, and the contemporary remains of the main temple of Ptah of Memphis.

At right angles to the main axis of the temple were built repository chapels, large and small, that served as resting places for the sacred barge during the processions. Other individual temple buildings were on north or south according to their relationship to the neighboring sanctuaries. The most important of these is the temple of the moon god Khonsu, child of Amon and Mut. It faces south toward the temple of Luxor, with which it was connected by an avenue of sphinxes well over a mile long. Its builder was Ramesses III. It is historically important for its good state of preservation and also for its systematic layout; in its succession of halls and their arrangements it continued to serve as a model until the temples of the Late Period. Passing through a portal between gate towers, one enters a court flanked by double porticoes. At the end of the court stands the temple porch at a slightly higher level. Next comes a broader hypostyle hall with a tall central aisle and lateral windows. The columns of the central aisle, like those of the great hypostyle hall at Karnak and the Ramesseum, have open papyrus blooms as capitals. Beyond this hall lies a square room with the barge chapel of the god in the middle. In the rear part of the temple is a

193. *Karnak, temple of Amon-Ra,
sacred lake, from south. Left to
right in background; pylon VII,
pylon I, great hypostyle hall,
obelisk of Hatshepsut.*

194. *Karnak, temple of Amon-Ra,
view toward south from pylon I:
great court with kiosk of Taharqa;
facade of temple of Ramesses III;
pylons VIII and IX on south axis.*

195. *Karnak, temple of Amon-Ra,
landing place and avenue of
sphinxes toward pylon I.*

broad low-pillared hall with chapels on three sides. These characteristic
features, which were already prepared for in the Eighteenth Dynasty in the
layout of the temple of Luxor, have been organized into a logical schema in
the temple of Khonsu. From one chamber to the next the floors are slightly
raised, the ceilings become lower in the same rhythm and the passages narrower. As one advances through the first pillared hall into the interior of
the building the light becomes steadily dimmer, first admitted through
lateral windows and then through mere slits in the roof. The sanctuary lies
in total darkness; it hides with its cult image the "secret" of the temple.

The Temple of Luxor
The temple of Luxor, on the south side of Thebes like the principal sanctuary of Karnak, also goes back to the Middle Kingdom. Under Hatshepsut
and Tuthmosis III a granite chapel stood there with well-proportioned
papyrus-bundle columns, incorporated by Ramesses II with the great court
he added on the north. The Luxor temple itself was the work of
Amenhotep III and was built according to a uniform plan and on a much
larger scale than the older sanctuary. It lies close to the Nile bank facing
north and was the "southern harem" of Amon, who was worshiped here as
the god of procreation. It thus had a particular significance for the king,
whose divine conception and birth are represented in the "birth room" on
the east side.

Unequaled in Egyptian architecture is the lofty elongated passage, with
its two rows of fifty-foot papyrus columns with open flowers for capitals,
that leads into the great court of the temple. No pylon towers emphasized
the entrance to this huge hall; no side aisles expanded it, as in the great
hypostyle hall at Karnak. It formed a monumental reception hall for
the king and the sacred barges, which paused here before crossing the wide
courtyard leading to the inner temple. The square open court with its
double rows of well-proportioned papyrus-bundle columns merges on the
south into the main entrance hall having columns of the same form. Crossing the "hall of offerings" one enters the barge sanctuary which, built
within an ambulatory, is distinguished as an independent structure by
fillets at the corners and crowning concave cornices. The rearmost
chambers of the temple are accessible only from the sides through a
transverse columned hall. They consist of a row of three chapels, the one in
the center being the holy of holies where the cult image of the sacred triad
stood on a pedestal.

In front of Amenhotep III's long entrance passage Ramesses II added
the already mentioned spacious court; its entrance, on the north, is guarded by a pylon and obelisks, and the facade faces toward Karnak, linked by
an avenue of sphinxes with Amon's main sanctuary.

The "Primeval Hill" at Medinet Habu
In addition to the temples of Karnak and Luxor on the east bank of the Nile

at Thebes, there is on the west bank a small but important sanctuary at Medinet Habu, south of the original city limits. As the "true center of primordial creation" this little temple could claim to be one of the holiest places of the holiest places of Thebes. Hatshepsut began its construction, over an older sanctuary, and it was revised and completed by her successor Tuthmosis III. The elongated rectangular building, whose ground plan is also recognizable in sanctuaries elsewhere, has rounded moldings at the four corners and is crowned above an upper encircling molding by a concave cornice. The whole stands on a moderately high podium reached by a small flight of steps on the east front. A canal branching from the Nile probably ended in front of the temple forecourt.

The building is divided into two different areas. In front of the customary sanctuary is a barge chapel of the "baldachin temple" type with pillars on three sides and waist-high walls between them; in the middle stands a long shrine for Amon's barge. Originally the ceiling of this shrine—evidently the archetypal sacred hut beneath an awning—was lower than the roof of the surrounding column structure. The rear part of the temple is enclosed by outer walls, and here the ceiling height is lower than in the front part. The structure contains several small chambers: on the central axis is a square room, the main chamber, for its ceiling is somewhat higher and has a light-slit directing a feeble beam of light onto a statuary group representing the god Amon and the king, of which remains have been preserved. The rooms lying south and west of the main chamber served the cult of Amon; the room on the north, accessible only from the barge chapel, served the cult of the king.

This sanctuary on the "primeval hill of Djeme" (Thebes) maintained close relations with the temple of Luxor on the east bank. At the beginning of each decade Amon was transported by barge, from his "southern harem," across to the temple on the west side of the river to make offerings to the "primordial gods." In the Twentieth Dynasty Ramesses III chose the immediate vicinity of this hallowed place to build his huge mortuary temple. He enclosed the ancient sanctuary within the fortress-like walls of his own temple area. The cult was maintained into the Ptolemaic era and during all this time the small Eighteenth Dynasty temple remained substantially untouched. Late inscriptions refer to the sanctuary as the "tomb of the eight original gods and the primeval snake Kneph," and accordingly various additions were made in the Thirtieth Dynasty and under the Ptolemies: entrance buildings, a hypostyle hall, pylons, and a small pillared entrance hall where the processions were ceremonially received.

The Mortuary Temple of Queen Hatshepsut

For Thebes, the early Eighteenth Dynasty was a genuinely creative period in architecture. The most important building of this period—surpassing all others in originality and boldness of conception, in the balance of its masses, in its climactic progress from entrance to holy of holies, and in

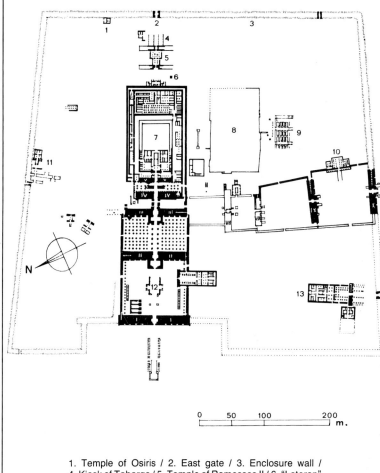

1. Temple of Osiris / 2. East gate / 3. Enclosure wall / 4. Kiosk of Taharqa / 5. Temple of Ramesses II / 6. "Lateran" obelisk / 7. Buildings of Tuthmosis III / 8. Sacred lake / 9. Buildings of Psamnut / 10. Temple of Amenhotep II / 11. Temple of Ptah / 12. Great court / 13. Temple of Khonsu.

199. *Karnak, temple of Amon-Ra, longitudinal section of great festival hall of Tuthmosis III (from Haeny, 1970).*

200, 201. *Karnak, temple of Amon-Ra, great festival hall of Tuthmosis III, with tent pole columns, from south. Eighteenth Dynasty, c. 1460 B.C.*

202. *Karnak, temple of Amon-Ra, great hypostyle hall from north, and obelisks of Tuthmosis I (left) and Hatshepsut (right).*

203. *Karnak, temple of Amon-Ra, transverse section of great hypostyle hall (from Haeny, 1970).*

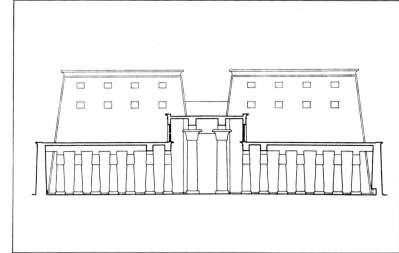

204. *Karnak, temple of Amon-Ra,* ▷ *south side of great hypostyle hall. Nineteenth Dynasty, c. 1290 B.C.*

205. *Karnak, temple of Amon-Ra,* ▷ *view toward south, through aisle of great hypostyle hall with ancient grille preserved. Nineteenth Dynasty, c. 1290 B.C.*

206. *Karnak, temple of Amon-Ra, view toward central aisle of great hypostyle hall. Nineteenth Dynasty, c. 1290 B.C.*

207. *Karnak, temple of Amon-Ra, obelisk of Tuthmosis I and central aisle of great hypostyle hall, from east.*

208. Karnak, temple of Khonsu,
porticoed court, from south.
Ramesses III, Twentieth Dynasty,
c. 1150 B.C.

wealth of statuary and reliefs—is the terraced temple of Queen Hatshepsut on the cliff valley at Deir el Bahari (the place takes its name from the Christian monastery called "northern monastery" that once nestled among the ruins). Hatshepsut has already been mentioned as a builder of the temple of Karnak. The temple at Deir el Bahari served not only for her own funerary cult and that of her father Tuthmosis I and of her husband Tuthmosis II, who died young, but was also dedicated to the cults of Amon, her divine begetter, and of other gods. In choosing the site the queen acknowledged the first political rise of Thebes in the Eleventh Dynasty, the proximity of Mentuhotep's mortuary temple, and the neighboring sanctuary of the goddess Hathor, guardian of the necropolis. The huge temple complex is the work of the architect Senmut, the queen's favorite, and it shows a solution that takes over from the earlier model only the outward-directed effect of its open galleries and additional influences from Twelfth Dynasty architecture of the Upper Egyptian nomarchs' tombs, with their numerous terraces clinging to the cliffs. All of those prototypes are wholly surpassed, and in the grandeur of the site, with its backdrop of majestic vertical cliffs, is proclaimed a totally new concept of the dignity of divine kingship.

The long sphinx-lined causeway leads from the rim of the cultivated land to the entrance portal, flanked by trees. The court extended, as with Mentuhotep's mortuary temple immediately to the south, in its full width of over 300 feet right up to the sanctuary, which rises in two giant steps and facing colonnades to the cliffs behind. These cliffs, soaring 350 almost vertical feet to a pyramidal peak, assumed the role of the missing pyramid. Into the other side of this mass of rock, from a spur of the Valley of the Kings, was tunneled the shaft leading to the tomb chamber of the queen, a distance of several hundred yards.

The broad court was planted with palm trees and grapevines. In front of the main structure ponds fringed with papyrus were laid out on either side of the center axis. Central ramps lead to the first and second terraces, and the buttressing walls are faced with colonnades of square pillars. Those of the lower colonnade, closing the court on the west, are decorated with the "Horus name" of the queen; this motif is continued on a giant scale along the outside of the niched buttressing wall that supports the second terrace on the south. The lower colonnade terminates at north and south in huge Osiris statues of the queen. The architectural decoration of the lower-story structures proclaims the royal name; on the next level the holiness of the precinct correspondingly rises, and on the outside faces of the pillars of the second colonnade the queen is shown before Amon. The sphere of the gods has begun; the second colonnade ends at the south in the chapel of the goddess Hathor, at the north in that of Anubis, god of the dead.

The Hathor chapel could also be reached by way of a separate ramp along the south buttressing wall. Its facade is formed by a row of square pillars between short end walls, identified as an independent building by its crowning cornice and rounded corner moldings. Inside, round columns

210. *Karnak, temple of Khonsu, outer face of access portal. Ptolemaic period, c. 220 B.C.*

211. *Karnak, temple of Khonsu, reliefs in access portal. Ptolemaic period, c. 220 B.C.*

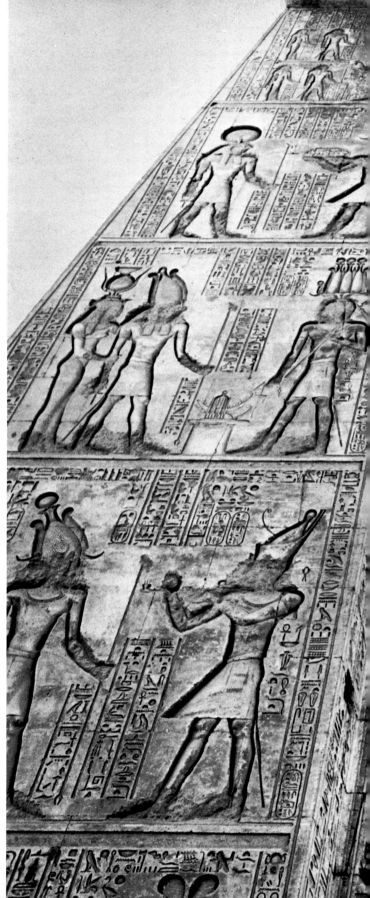

212. *Luxor, temple of Amenhotep III, from north; colonnaded passage and great court. Eighteenth Dynasty, c. 1370 B.C.*

with Hathor-head capitals divide the anteroom of the chapel into several aisles, and through the aisle between the central row of columns was accessible the holy of holies, carved out of the rock at the end. Even this rock-cut sanctuary of the goddess Hathor is identified as a separate building by the relief decoration on its entrance portal, in this case a tentlike Upper Egyptian shrine. The slender fluted supports with small Hathor-head capitals and apotropaic horns, which bear a flattened vaulted roof, and the decorative loops of the matting walls of a tent structure, recall a type similar to the dummy buildings in King Zoser's burial precinct. The Anubis chapel at the north end of the upper colonnade is also treated as an independent building. On the facade of the anteroom and within, the sixteen-sided fluted columns on low round bases stand out from the square pillars of the main colonnade. In this chapel, too, the holy of holies is carved out of the same cliffs; the walls and vaulted ceiling, as in all the rock-cut chambers, are faced with stone slabs and richly decorated with painted reliefs. The vault is painted with golden stars in a night-blue sky.

The curve of the vaulted ceilings, employed in Egyptian stone architecture since the Fifth Dynasty pyramids, was obtained by cutting off the projecting edges of layers of stone, and these ceilings seem to have signified the crossing over from this world to the next. Brick barrel vaults and domes over small square chambers were already familiar to the builders of the Fourth Dynasty, who used them in the annexes to stone mastabas. The segmental arch first appears in stone architecture in the eighth century B.C. But apart from its use in the inner chambers of sanctuaries in the specified Old Kingdom pyramid temples, and in the rock-cut chapels and a few other rare instances, the vault played no part in Egyptian sacred architecture; where it was used it could never be discerned from the outward appearance of a sacred building.

At the northeast corner of the Anubis chapel the cliff makes a sharp turn forward and forms the northern boundary of the terrace. Here too a shallow colonnade makes a facing for the cliff wall.

The second ramp leads to the uppermost terrace, the culmination of the sanctuary. A long solemn row of identical Osiris statues of the queen forms the facade fronting the square pillars of the main hall. In the center of the facade a granite portal leads into a narrow open court that is ringed by deep colonnaded halls. Recent examinations of this structure, which is in an advanced state of ruin, indicate that the row of pillars bordering the court was somewhat raised above the others. Immediately to the north of this courtyard area is a small open court where the sun god was worshiped at a great open-air altar that faced the rising sun; across from this sun sanctuary, to the south, is a group of vaulted chambers for the funerary cult of the queen and her ancestors. The holy of holies, dedicated to the god Amon, was carved out of the western cliff, exactly on the main axis of the temple and reached from the central court. Originally there were two chambers, one behind the other, but under the Ptolemies a third was added for the worship of two

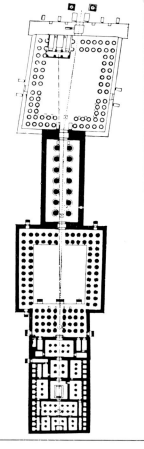

213. *Luxor, plan of temple of Amenhotep III (from Borchardt, 1896).*

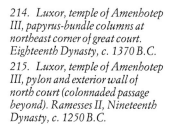

214. *Luxor, temple of Amenhotep III, papyrus-bundle columns at northeast corner of great court. Eighteenth Dynasty, c. 1370 B.C.*

215. *Luxor, temple of Amenhotep III, pylon and exterior wall of north court (colonnaded passage beyond). Ramesses II, Nineteenth Dynasty, c. 1250 B.C.*

216. *Luxor, temple of Amenhotep III, entrance pylon with obelisk and colossi of Ramesses II. Nineteenth Dynasty, c. 1250 B.C.*

217. Luxor, temple of Amenhotep
III, view from court of Ramesses II
to colonnaded passage of
Amenhotep III. Eighteenth-
Nineteenth Dynasties, c. 1370-
c. 1250 B.C.

great mortals: Imhotep, King Zoser's architect, inventor of stone architecture and author of a treatise on the planning of temples; and Amenhotep, son of Hapu, the architect of Amehotep III. For their wisdom, these architects were worshiped as gods: Senmut, architect of the terraced temple and favorite of Queen Hatshepsut, was long forgotten.

The terraced temple of Deir el Bahari is a remarkable example of the aesthetic adaptation of a building to its natural setting. Architecture, however, is always the product of a shaping intelligence and must assert its forms against the chaotic formlessness of nature. Small as compared with the towering crags against which it is built, Hatshepsut's temple occupies only the lower zone of the wall of cliffs. Yet the crisp horizontals of its terraces and the strict verticals of its colonnades differentiate it sharply from the rugged terrain, with which it is nonetheless intimately, though not visibly, connected by the sanctuaries hewn out of the living rock. The natural grandeur of the landscape has been incorporated with the temple's thematic function as the eternal seat of the godhead and as the burial place of the queen deep within the mountain.

The Amarna Period

The principle for the planning of the national sanctuary of the universal god Amon-Ra at Karnak, at the beginning of the Eighteenth Dynasty, was based on the worship of the sun god in open courts guarded at front and back by pylons and obelisks, as exemplified by the scant remains of the temple at Heliopolis. This principle can be recognized in the ancient core of the Karnak temple complex, as well as in the later additions on the south and west. The perpetual renewal of the kingship through the jubilee festival had a close association with the sun god—already confirmed in the Fifth Dynasty sun sanctuary, in the rich relief cycles of a "jubilee chamber" south of the great obelisk; and the idea of legitimate dynastic continuity, in the sense of the renewed conception of kingship, provided the stimulus for continual expansion through developing, enlarging, and improving the efficacy of the national shrine.

Thus, it was not in itself surprising that Amenhotep IV, successor of Amenhotep III, should have built, still under his original name, two separate temples for Ra-Harakhte, the sun god of Heliopolis, one east of Karnak, the other near Luxor. To judge from the partially cleared remains at Karnak—those at Luxor have not yet been excavated—these temples, too, appear to have consisted of large courts for the open-air worship of the day star. Amenhotep IV resided for about five years in the capital city of Thebes, before his personally propagated theology of the sun as "Aten" (the solar disk) took a turn so one-sided and so hostile to Amon that the king changed his own name from Amenhotep ("Amon is satisfied") to Akhenaten ("In the service of Aten"). He deserted Thebes, and banned and persecuted the cult of Amon. On virgin land in Middle Egypt, untrammeled by religious traditions of any kind, he founded his new capital,

218. *Medinet Habu (West Thebes) interior face of High Gate, southeast precinct gate of mortuary temple of Ramesses III. Twentieth Dynasty, c. 1150 B.C.*

219. *Medinet Habu (West Thebes), reconstruction of High Gate, southeast precinct gate of mortuary temple of Ramesses III. Twentieth Dynasty, c. 1150 B.C. (from Holscher, 1933).*

Akhetaten ("The horizon of Aten"), on the east bank of the Nile opposite the ancient site of Hermopolis. After a mere twelve years this royal residence and exclusive cult center of the sole god proclaimed by the king fell into decay, following the collapse of the new belief and the king's death, and shortly it was razed with all its buildings and sanctuaries to obliterate all memory of the "heretic." Excavations at the site thus reveal little more than the foundations of the palaces, temples, and living quarters, whose original buildings have been to some extent reconstructed with the aid of contemporary reliefs discovered in the tombs nearby.

Like the visage of the new god, the planning of his temples at Akhetaten can be linked with the Heliopolitan model. The common theme was an axial succession of pylon-fronted courts, where on innumerable altars in the open air the king and his family offered sacrifices to the sun. Statues of the king placed against pillars, as in the open areas of the temple of Karnak, stood around the courts as witnesses to his presence and to the perpetual renewal of his claim to kingship. The architects of the Amarna period consistently translated the religious ideas propounded by the king himself into a succession of new architectural forms. These include many appurtenances of the temples (whose thematic significance is still not clearly understood), the erection of columns in front of pylons to form vestibules flanking the entrances, and especially the temple gates to the sanctuaries. In the theology of the new sun cult, the display of the gloom of the Underworld had no longer a place, and now even shadow was to be shunned. The temple gates had lintels broken back in the middle and cropped on either side, so that the king could pass through in unbroken sunlight. Temple approaches continued to be treated in this way to the very end of Egyptian architecture; they made it possible to carry the emblems of the gods in procession into the interior of the temples without lowering them at the entrance.

After the collapse of Amenhotep IV's religious reformation, Thebes ceased to be country's political capital; however, it remained the religious center of the restored cult of Amon and, until the end of the New Kingdom, the burial place of the kings. The royal mortuary temples, the kings' "houses for millions of years," were ranged at the foot of the western hills, but the great experiment of Hatshepsut's terraced temple was nowhere adopted. Of the mortuary temples of the queen's immediate successors only that of Tuthmosis III has been thoroughly explored; although it is on a more modest scale, the two share certain features, for example, a Hathor chapel on the south side. From Amenhotep III's huge mortuary complex, all that remains are the enthroned colossi, sixty-five feet high and made of quartzite that the king's architect, Amenhotep, son of Hapu, ordered from the quarries near Heliopolis, some 300 miles north of Thebes. At one time they flanked the monumental entrance with its massive pylon towers. The later mortuary temples (insofar as they still

stand)—of Sety I in the northern section of the necropolis, of Ramesses II (Ramesseum), and of Ramesses III at Medinet Habu—appear to have been planned according to the principle of successive spaces at the temple of Luxor. The temple is usually approached through two sets of pylons, each leading into a broad court. A vestibule on the west side of the second court leads to the hypostyle hall, which may be followed by various smaller pillared halls, and finally to the sanctuary. A separate chapel is reserved for the royal ancestors. The main sanctuary is solely for the cult of Amon and the king. The sun god also has a private chapel within the temple. Along the main axis the sequence of rooms is fixed; the side rooms and the arrangements at the rear of the temple follow the cult requirements imposed by the royal builder.

In the back area of the Ramesseum huge brick-built store-rooms and offices for the administration of the temple have been preserved. Each chamber is covered by a barrel vault. After the end of the Eighteenth Dynasty, when Thebes was no longer a royal residence, a small palace was built on the south side of the first court of the ruler's mortuary temple for his occasional visits at the time of the great festivals.

As cult places for the king and the gods, the mortuary temples were enclosed by high walls like the sanctuaries of the gods, with pylons forming the monumental front entrance. Ramesses III, developing the idea of the temple as a "fortress of the god" but certainly also mindful of the internal political difficulties of the Twentieth Dynasty, enclosed his funerary temple within double battlemented walls with massive tower-like fortress gates on east and west. In front of the east gate was a landing place for a canal leading from the Nile. Despite its fortified aspect, emphasized by the triumphal reliefs decorating the exterior, the upper chambers of the towers served as a "pleasure pavilion" for the king and his daughters, who are represented on the walls in reliefs of intimate scenes.

The Cliff Temple of Abu Simbel

Nubia had been an Egyptian province since the beginning of the New Kingdom. Temple buildings in a purely Egyptian style secured the land in the name of Egyptian gods and kings. The most important of these temples was that built by Ramesses II on a bend in the Nile at Abu Simbel. On the west bank the high ground runs directly down to the river, forming a steep cliff. As at Deir el Bahari on the west bank at Thebes, here too the cliff itself was sacred. Ramesses transformed it into a temple. Within a trapezoidal area are four colossal statues of the enthroned king, the whole carved from the wall of sandstone cliffs to resemble the front of a pylon. The paired statues flank the entrance portal, which is oriented precisely east toward the sunrise. Above the portal in a niche is the figure of Ra-Harakhte of Heliopolis, the falcon-headed sun god. The upper termination of the "pylon" front is formed by a row of baboons, their arms raised to hail the rising run. The arrangement of the inner rooms, which penetrate deep

221, 222. *Abu Simbel, facade of great rock temple and four colossi of Ramesses II (as relocated). Nineteenth Dynasty, c. 1250 B.C.*

223. Abu Simbel, interior of great rock temple of Ramesses II, lateral view of royal statues before pillars. Nineteenth Dynasty, c. 1250 B.C.

XXI. Karnak, temple of Amon-Ra, great festival hall of Tuthmosis III.

XXII. Karnak, temple of Amon-Ra, hypostyle hall and obelisks of Tuthmosis I and Queen Hatshepsut.

XXIII. *Edfu, temple of Horus.*

224. *Abu Simbel, interior of great rock temple of Ramesses II, frontal view of royal statues before pillars. Nineteenth Dynasty, c. 1250 B.C.*

into the side of the cliff, corresponds to the plan of the Theban temples. The great rock-cut hall that one first enters after passing through the entrance portal is the counterpart of the temple court. Standing figures of Ramesses II in festival attire are ranged in front of the pillars. Next follows a square hypostyle hall and a wider chamber, with the holy of holies beyond the center of its innermost wall. The shrine, moved now to higher ground, contains a group of four seated statues representing Amon-Ra of Thebes, Ra-Harakhte of Heliopolis, Ptah of Memphis, and the king himself, all of whom were worshiped here.

An unusual feature of this temple is the presence of narrow compartments at right angles on either side of the main halls. These were probably treasure chambers, repositories for Nubian gold.

The Temple and Cenotaph of Sety I at Abydos

Egyptian architecture was chiefly preoccupied with the expression of eternal verities in material form, and the unusual temple of Sety I at Abydos illustrates this concern impressively. Abydos, the Upper Egyptian burial place of the early kings, had become in the Old Kingdom the home and sanctuary of the god Osiris. As vegetation god and divine ruler of the mythical past, Osiris was closely associated with the question of legitimate succession. In death the king suffered the fare of the god, to be summoned like him to rule over the world of the dead; the king's son and heir, identified with Osiris' son Horus, was the earthly ruler. Osiris, who came originally from the Delta (Busiris), had since the Old Kingdom taken over the seat of the god of the dead and the cult place of the "Foremost of the Westerners." His burial place was believed to have been found at Abydos in what was, in fact, the tomb of a First Dynasty king, and his death and return to life were dramatically celebrated in mystery plays enacted along the path that stretched from the city temple to the ancient royal necropolis. Abydos became a center of pilgrimage; kings and private individuals built cenotaphs along the processional route of the mystery plays to ensure themselves a share in the blessings of this holy place.

Like all the kings of the New Kingdom, Sety I had his burial place at Thebes, in the Valley of the Kings, although for strategic reasons he had established his residence at Kantir in the eastern Delta. His mortuary temple, in part well preserved, is the northernmost of those on the Theban west bank. In the Theban mortuary temples the worship of Amon-Ra as the universal god, and the dogma of his having fathered the king, had driven the older god Osiris into the background. The Nineteenth Dynasty first brought back shrines dedicated to the god of the dead, of vegetation, and of the rulers.

Thus Sety I returned to earlier beliefs when at Abydos he built an important westward-oriented temple with two pylons, two courts, and an interior laid out according to the Theban plan. The aisles through a rising sequence of pillared and columned halls lead to seven chapels; the central

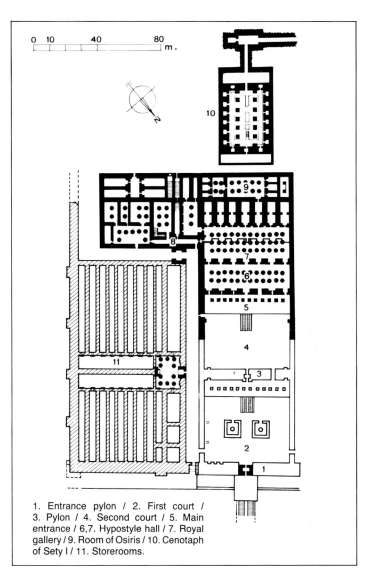

1. Entrance pylon / 2. First court / 3. Pylon / 4. Second court / 5. Main entrance / 6,7. Hypostyle hall / 7. Royal gallery / 9. Room of Osiris / 10. Cenotaph of Sety I / 11. Storerooms.

one, dedicated to the national god Amon-Ra, is flanked by those of Ra-Harakhte and Osiris. The south wing contains the chapels of the king and the Memphite god Ptah, the north those of Isis and Horus, wife and son of Osiris. These elongated chapels, except for that of Osiris, had vaulted ceilings. A false door was represented in the westward-facing rear walls; false doors signified that behind them lay something involved in the cult. Only the Osiris chapel has a real door. This leads to chambers, dedicated to the cult of the god and his family, that form a narrow transept at the back of the seven chapels.

Reliefs on the temple walls depict the shrine, barge, and cult images, and the rites performed by the king; they are invaluable for recreating the former appearance of the temple and determining the functions of its various parts. The unusual annex on the south side of the main building contained chapels for other gods and the shrine of Sety's ancestors, who are listed by name, from Menes (Narmer), the founder of the kingdom, to the builder of the temple himself.

The cenotaph of Sety I lies just to the southwest on the axis of the main temple; it is important for the architectural history of this complex. A structure sunk deep in the ground, its roof lay below the floor level of the main temple and its core was built entirely of massive granite blocks. Originally it was an isolated building; there is a separate access at the northeast end which, however, is interrupted by a deep shaft. The core of this cenotaph forms a rectangular chamber with a platform occupying the middle, surrounded by a moat that was filled with water by the annual Nile floods. On the short sides there are steps leading down to the level reached by the water.

In the middle of the "island" two recesses for the sarcophagus and the canopic shrine are still visible. Two rows of stout granite pillars on the long sides support giant longitudinal architraves on which rested the ceiling blocks of the roof; these were probably corbeled toward the center, forming a barrel vault above the center of the platform. The walls surrounding this entire space contain niches whose significance is still uncertain. The use of undecorated massive granite blocks recalls the architecture of the Fourth Dynasty mortuary temples at Giza.

The location and organization of this building leave no doubt that it was a cenotaph of the builder at the place most sacred to Osiris. The inner "island" symbolizes the "primeval hill" emerging from the waters of chaos to indicate the beginning of self-perpetuating creation. Simultaneously the island tomb equates the king with the god Osiris; according to ancient belief Osiris lay buried on an island which, on the one hand, represented the "pure" and "unapproachable," and on the other, symbolically linked his death and resurrection with the cyclical rise and fall of the Nile. Later representations show a sacred grove planted over Sety's subterranean building so that its shadow would envelop the soul of the dead king while its plants simultaneously honored Osiris as the creator of vegetation.

THE ARCHITECTURE OF THE LATE PERIOD

The end of the New Kingdom was followed by political debility, domestic turmoil and impoverishment, pressures from without, and foreign rule, and during these times the opportunities for Egyptian architecture diminished. There were frequent shifts of the capital, mostly within Lower Egypt. Memphis rose repeatedly to prominence, but there and throughout the Delta virtually nothing has survived to supplement the buildings of the Late Period that still stand in Upper Egypt.

The occasional partitioning of the country and the frequent changes of dynasty weakened and secularized the kingship. No extensive royal tombs survive, not even those of the native kings from Sais, Mendes, and Sebennytos in the Delta. According to Herodotus, the kings of the Twenty-Sixth Dynasty, like those of the Twenty-First Dynasty at Tanis, were buried according to ancient Lower Egyptian custom within the temple precincts of the local deity. The Egyptianized Ethiopian kings of the Twenty-Fifth Dynasty, in their capital of Napata below the fourth cataract, were buried in small, very steep pyramids with a mortuary chapel on the east side.

The kings of the Ptolemaic dynasty, the successors of Alexander the Great, resided in their newly founded, purely Hellenistic capital of Alexandria, where they were buried in tombs of which nothing has been preserved.

Throughout and after the first millennium B.C. native and foreign rulers alike continued to assume the ancient role of the Pharaohs. The basic Egyptian concept of the king ruling with the god in the interests of world order continued to be preserved, at least as a fiction. The maintenance and embellishment of the famous old sanctuaries and the erection of new temples continued to be a royal obligation. Wearing pharaonic regalia Ethiopians, Persian kings, Macedonians, and Roman emperors appear in reliefs and inscriptions venerating the Egyptian gods and confirming the god-given cosmic order in the prescribed rites. Pomp and ritual establishes inwardly and outwardly their legitimate royal claim by way of the old forms of architecture, reliefs faithfully reproduced, and statues following the Egyptian canon.

The building activities in the Nile Valley of the Ethiopians, the Saitic dynasty, and the Persians are hardly noteworthy. Large-scale building throughout the country was resumed only under the kings of the Thirtieth Dynasty. The Ptolemies completed temples already begun, such as Nectanebo II's temple of Isis built all of granite in the Delta—the celebrated Iseum of Roman times, later destroyed by an earthquake and today only an imposing heap of ruins. The Ptolemies and Romans built temples throughout Egypt, including Nubia; preference was given to places that had special political and religious importance in maintaining the accustomed order and legitimate rule. The large temples of Upper Egypt stand on hallowed ground and, appealing to the oldest traditions, were rebuilt over

228. *Edfu, birth house in front of temple of Horus. Ptolemaic period, 237-57 B.C.*

229. *Edfu, plan of temple of Horus (from Baedeker, 1928).*

230. *Edfu, pylon of temple ▷ of Horus. Ptolemaic period, 237-57 B.C.*

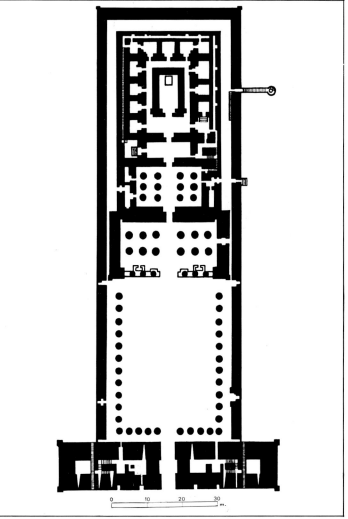

ancient sanctuaries which they far outstripped in size and splendor. The most important and best preserved are at Dendera, Esna, Edfu, Kom Ombo, Philae, and, among the Nubian temples, Kalabsha. Architecturally each temple has a marked individuality determined by the local tradition of its principal deity and subsidiary cults, and each makes an appeal through inscriptions to a venerable history reaching back to the age of myth and the days when the country was first united.

The orientation of the temples is determined by their particular location on the east or west bank and by the usually north-south course of the river. The clear axial arrangement and spatial succession, extending from entrance portal to holy of holies, divides the temple into two halves, one on the north, one on the south, whose plan and arrangements correspond to one another in their inscriptions. There is regularly a canal leading from the Nile to the temple precincts furthest inland. The traditional festivals, in which, for example, Hathor of Dendera visited Horus of Edfu in his temple almost one hundred miles up the Nile, required these waterways for transporting the cult image on the sacred barge.

The temple precincts were always sheltered from the impure world outside by high brick walls and were entered through monumental stone portals. One such portal, dating from Ptolemaic times, has been preserved at Karnak. The sacred enclosure included the temple of the principal deity, the sacred lake, a well (whose water level simultaneously indicated the state of the Nile), the smaller sanctuaries of lesser gods, and, after the fourth century B.C., the "birth house," usually situated to one side of the main entrance facing the approaches to the temple.

A new, lively, and especially versatile element, characteristic of the temples since the fourth century B.C., is the column capital. From the older plant-form columns late temple architecture retains only the palm and lotus columns in their original form; no use is made of the various older forms of pillars. The new capitals all develop from the papyrus plant in bloom. Two basic forms may be distinguished: first, the full-blown bell-shaped papyrus capital decorated with vertical plant ribs, leaves, and floral ornament in finely graded relief; second, large semicircular papyrus blooms arranged to form a circle in the upper part and interlaced below with smaller blooms, composing a sort of bouquet. These forms have many variants and the capitals may change within the same building or even from column to column within the same row.

The Temple of Horus at Edfu
To describe the oldest and largest of these Ptolemaic temples, the temple of Horus at Edfu, is in a sense to describe them all. The construction took about 180 years (237-57 B.C.). The massive pylons and main gate of the pylons, form the side walls of the great court, and enclose the temple face south. High stone walls with concave and roll moldings on the outside abut against the backs of the temple structure on the other three sides. The

231. *Edfu, pylon and enclosure wall of Temple of Horus, from southwest. Ptolemaic period, 237-57 B.C.*

232. *Edfu, temple of Horus, view through "hall of appearances" toward sanctuary. Ptolemaic period, 237-57 B.C.*

233. Edfu, court of temple
of Horus. Ptolemaic period,
237-57 B.C.

234. Edfu, temple of Horus, enclosure wall (right) and temple wall (left), from north. Ptolemaic period, 237-57 B.C.

235. Edfu, temple of Horus, western stairway on roof. Ptolemaic period, 237-57 B.C.

court, "the hall of the masses," was open to the people. Porticoes, their architraves surmounted by concave and roll moldings, surround it on east, west, and south (including the side backing the pylons), stopping just short of the actual temple.

The main temple building is divided clearly into two parts, differentiated by unequal height, width, and depth. Fronting on the court is the great hypostyle hall, a broader and taller "antechamber" to the closed, elongated sanctuary behind.

The intercolumniations of the facade, apart from the central portal with its cropped architrave and doors that could be closed, are filled by stone screens half the height of the column shafts and preventing a view of the interior. These screens are edged with fillets and crowned by a concave molding with a uraeus frieze; their outer faces are decorated with reliefs. They are derived ultimately from the mats stretched between the fluted posts of tent structures, reproduced in stone in King Zoser's mortuary precinct. As an architectonic element with concave and roll moldings they are first represented in the smalll chapel in a New Kingdom tomb, and they appear in stone construction in the Twenty-Second Dynasty temple of Amon, built at el-Hibe in Middle Egypt.

The great hypostyle hall, like an independent building, has torus moldings at the four outer corners, at the top of the outer walls, and above the architraves in the facade, and the whole is crowned by a massive cornice. Its floor is one step above the level of the court. Built onto the back of one of the screens of the front colonnade is the library, whose catalogue of papyrus rolls is recorded on the inner walls of the small chamber. The hypostyle hall is a special feature of the temple; at Dendera the hypostyle hall was added in Roman times to the already-completed temple.

The front of the narrower and lower temple block overlaps with the rear wall of the great hypostyle hall. On the axis of the temple, a monumental portal closed with two huge doors leads into the "hall of appearances," which is narrower than the full width of the temple; its ceiling rests on columns.

When the doors were closed this hall, and indeed the whole interior of the temple proper, lay in darkness; only narrow slits in the ceiling admitted occasional dim light. In the "hall of appearances" was displayed the cult image, together with those of the lesser gods also worshiped in the temple; here the processions were organized on festival days. The hall is flanked by smaller chambers where the unguents for the cult image were prepared and the temple treasures stored. A small door led out to the well that supplied the pure water needed in the daily ritual.

The next chamber is also a transept hall, but without columns; it is the "hall of offerings" where three times each day the food offered to the god was served and consecrated. On both sides of the "hall of offerings" narrow steps lead up to the roof; one goes upward in a single straight flight, and the other, four flights of gentler steps arranged around a square, was for

236. Dendera, facade of temple of Hathor, from northeast. Late Ptolemaic-Roman period.

237, 238. Dendera, exterior of temple of Hathor, from west and south. Late Ptolemaic-Roman period.

239. Dendera, temple of Hathor, slits for illumination in ceiling of hypostyle hall. Late Ptolemaic-Roman period.

coming down. On the side walls are reliefs depicting processions, the gods going up or down according to the design of the stair.

Beyond the "hall of offerings" begins the holy of holies, which, with its accompanying chapels, occupies the entire rear part of the temple. It begins with the "middle hall," also referred to in the inscriptions as the "hall of the multiplicity of gods." This chamber forms at the same time the threshold to the sanctuary; the floor rises, and the shrine of the principal god turns its narrow face and closing doors to the entering worshiper. Here, before the sanctuary, appeared the other gods worshiped in the temple, to protect and defend the main god. Again two small chambers open off either side of the hall: that on the west preserved the wardrobe of the god, that on the east led to a small sanctuary with a little open court, from which steps rise to the "pure chapel" at a higher level. On the occasion of the New Year festival the cult image was anointed, clothed, and crowned in this chapel before being conveyed in solemn procession to the roof.

The sanctuary—the "holy of holies," the "throne room"—of the principal god is an elongated freestanding structure, and as such is architecturally differentiated: a narrow passage surrounds it on three sides. Opening onto this passage are the chapels of the secondary gods; only the center chapel behind the sanctuary is dedicated to a special form of the principal god.

It has already been mentioned that there were ascending and descending processions from the "hall of offerings" to the flat roof. The roof of the temple was not, however, all in one plane; the roof level from the "hall of appearances" to the sanctuary area was higher than that above the smaller rooms and chapels at the sides and rear. The lower levels of the roof were screened from view by the high outer wall of the temple. During the New Year festival this particular area of the roof, accessible from the stairways, had a vital function to perform: the cult image was conveyed in solemn procession to the roof where its potency was renewed by exposing it in a special roof chapel to the rays of the rising sun. At Edfu the location and plan of this chapel can still be discerned on the roof of the temple; at Dendera, on the southwest corner of the roof, the chapel itself is preserved. On the roof of Dendera there are also separate chambers for the Osiris cult.

A special feature of the great temples of the Late Period is their systems of "crypts." These are narrow chambers beneath the floor of the foundations or in the thick outside walls around the holy of holies. Their location was known only to the initiated and they could be entered only by removing a stone slab. They provided safe storage for the costly votive gifts, emblems of the gods, and ritual objects in gold and silver which are listed on the walls and depicted in relief. Sometimes the crypts were at several levels, one below the other. Their concealed locations recall the story of the treasure chambers of Rhampsinit told us by Herodotus (*Histories,* II, 121).

At the side before the entrance pylon to the temple of Edfu stands the birth house (Mammisi). These small temples, always present in the great

241-243. *Dendera, pavilion on roof of temple of Hathor. Late Ptolemaic-Roman period.*

sanctuaries of the Late Period, have the form of a chapel with peripteral columns bearing a sundeck. On certain festivals they were the scene of liturgical celebrations of the god and of the birth of the king. Unknown before the fourth century B.C., they emphasize the theme of the "divine child" and the "divine mother." The walled chapel within, which is treated as an isolated building, has the entrance at the front, made lower to conform with the "baldachin temple" prototype. The stone roof-slabs of the exterior gallery rest on the architraves spanning tall columns and on the walls of the chapel inside. Screens block the spaces between the columns, extending halfway up the shafts; they are decorated with reliefs depicting the adoration of the cult of the divine mother and her child. Often above the capital is another block bearing the grotesque figure of Bes, the popular demon who watched over mother and child.

The Temple of Hathor at Dendera

After the temple of Horus at Edfu, the next most important and best-preserved of the Ptolemaic temples is that of the goddess Hathor at Dendera, begun in 80 B.C. According to the inscriptions the founding of the historic sanctuary goes back to the period of unification of the Two Lands, and King Cheops is mentioned as one of the restorers. As with all Egyptian temples, construction began with the holy of holies and ended with the entrance and the great hypostyle hall, which at Dendera dates only from the reign of Augustus. The ceiling of the hypostyle hall rests on columns with four-sided Hathor-sistrum capitals. The succession of main rooms and subordinate chambers at Dendera corresponds almost exactly with that of the temple of Horus at Edfu. Again there are two stairways leading to the roof. The reliefs on the staircase walls depict the costumes of the members of the procession in scrupulous detail: the gods, warding off enemies, march in front; behind the emblem of the temple there follow the king and the priests with the emblems of the gods; then comes the queen with each hand swinging the sistrum, the cult symbol of Hathor; next the priests bearing Hathor's image in its shrine; closing the procession are the lesser gods of the temple.

At the southwest corner of the roof stands the goal of the procession, a kiosk with twelve Hathor columns. The roof of this small building was, as representations show, once covered with a low vault; to judge from the traces of its construction left on the walls, it must have been made of wood.

The temple precinct of Dendera is still surrounded today by a thick brick wall and entered through the ancient portal. The original birth house, dating from the Thirtieth Dynasty, was later cut through by the stone enclosure wall of the temple; the emperor Augustus therefore had a new one built near the entrance to the precinct. Close to the southwest corner of the Hathor temple lies the sacred lake, enclosed by walls and with steps at each corner that led down to the former water level. Alongside the south runs a narrow landing place, probably used in connection with the Osiris festival.

The Temple of Mandulis at Kalabsha

The temple at Kalabsha in Nubia, on the west bank of the Nile some forty miles south of Aswan, was probably built under Cleopatra and Caesar. Well preserved, easily comprehended, and carefully composed in its relation of masses, it gives a clear idea of the latest Egyptian temple architecture. The sanctuary is dedicated to the Nubian god Mandulis. The landing place for the sacred barge is in an especially good state of preservation. The two pylon towers and the side walls of the court contain a great number of small chambers, a feature of this temple. The slight deviation of the pylons from the temple axis, necessitated by the proximity of the river, is cleverly compensated by shortening one of the towers. While the ground plan corresponds in principle to those of other temples, it has been considerably simplified. The temple proper contains only three rooms, all at right angles to the main axis, the last one forming the sanctuary. All three receive dim light from slits in the ceiling and in the upper part of the walls. The ceiling height decreases substantially in the direction of the holy of holies, and the doorways grow proportionately smaller. The remains of a well are in the narrow passage between the temple building and the enclosure wall.

The proportions of this temple are rather unusual; the ratio of length to breadth is 200 to 100 feet. The temple would have been drowned in the waters of the lake created by the new Aswan High Dam had it not been dismantled under the supervision of scholars, stone by stone, and rebuilt on higher ground. During the dismantling there came to light the outline grid of the planning and the preliminary drawing, scored in the flat surface of the rock foundation. This carved outline was probably transferred to the site from a small-scale drawing. The long sides are divided into sixteen parts, the short sides into eleven: the grid therefore did not consist of squares, as is assumed to have been the case with the older Egyptian temples. The grid also contains proportional elevations of the facades of the first hypostyle hall and the sanctuary.

The Island of Philae

One of the most important cult and pilgrimage centers of the Ptolemaic and Roman periods was the island of Philae, just south of the first cataract. To judge from the extant buildings and the religious traditions, the island did not become one of Egypt's famous holy places until relatively late, in the midfourth century B.C. The establishing of the sanctuaries on the island brought together the religious and political ideas of the Ptolemaic and the Roman periods. Philae lay in the border zone between Egypt and Nubia. In this region the worship of Isis and Osiris, the popular universal gods of the Late Period, had taken hold, displacing the older cults on the island of Elephantine near Aswan. The Osiris tomb or "abaton" on Bige, a small rocky islet west of Philae, and Philae itself surpassed in holiness even Abydos as a center of the death ceremonies of Osiris. Here, according to late theology, the Nile with its annual fecundating flood had its source in a

245. *Dendera, sacred lake of temple of Hathor. Late Ptolemaic-Roman period.*

cave in which one of the Osiris relics was kept. The motherly Isis and her son Horus were also venerated in Nubia and by the nomads of the eastern desert, the Blemmyes. During the centuries of conflict between Egypt and the south, Philae and its sanctuaries remained an island of peace. Shrines of the Nubian divinities joined those of the Egyptian gods. Even Mandulis, the local god of Kalabsha, had a temple there. Thus the little island, only a quarter of a mile long and barely two hundred yards wide, became a temple city.

The Temple of Isis was the principal sanctuary, and still stands on the west side of the island; next to the Iseum in the Delta, it was the most important center for the worship of the goddess. The siting of the other sanctuaries, built here between the fourth century B.C. and the second century A.D., was determined by the north-south orientation of the Isis temple, the processional way of her sacred image, the cult relations with the Osiris tomb on nearby Bige, and the rocky topography of Philae itself.

The approach to the Temple of Isis lay at the southwest corner of the island where Nectanebo II, the last native ruler of Egypt, built a reception hall. The processional way leading northward to the temple was bordered on both sides by long columned halls; the western one followed the shore, the eastern one was backed by smaller shrines. Compared with the great temples of the Late Period at Edfu and Dendera the Isis temple is small, but it is unsurpassed in quality of execution. The first pylon leads into the court, closed on the north by a second pylon. The western boundary of the court is formed by the birth house, which here—like the main sanctuary—is oriented north-south and has its own entrance from the west tower of the first pylon. Opposite the birth house are the rooms for the preparation of the ritual unguents, and a library; these close off the court on the east. Directly in back of the second, smaller pylon is the great columned vestibule of the temple; to light this hall a small area near the front was left unroofed. The "hall of appearances" follows, with a stairway on the west side leading to the roof. On the east side, as in the temples at Edfu and Dendera, there is a tiny court and the "pure chapel" for the New Year festival. Beyond the "hall of appearances" lies the "middle hall," and against the rear wall of the temple stand three sanctuaries side by side. As at Dendera, the chapel for the celebration of the rebirth of Osiris is on the roof.

The emperor Hadrian's pavilion, in our picture, partly concealed by the big south pylon, remained unfinished; standing on the higher ground along the eastern shoreline of the island, it probably served as a way-station chapel for the festival processions. Like the pavilion on the roof of the temple of Dendera this building, surrounded by tall screened columns, once had a low rounded wooden roof.

The ancient quay walls that bordered the island are in great part preserved, especially on the southwest; they still create the impression that is compared in a contemporary inscription to a mighty "ship."

181

246. *Kalabsha, temple of Mandulis, facade of vestibule. Roman period-beginning of Christian era.*

247. *Kalabsha, temple of Mandulis, from southwest. Roman period-beginning of Christian era.*

248. *Kalabsha, temple of Mandulis (as relocated) with pavilion of Kertassi. Roman period-beginning of Christian era.*

Philae was the last refuge of the pagan cults. Even in the fifth century A.D., when the Nile Valley was Christianized and the temples of the pharaonic past had long been closed, Philae's temples continued to be used by the warlike tribes of Nubia and the eastern desert. Before the first dam was constructed south of Aswan—creating a reservoir that submerged the island and its buildings for much of the year—Philae was one of the unspoilt places where the Nile, flowing through the barren rocky landscape, combined with the ancient buildings to create an atmosphere in which the presence and potency of the gods could still be felt.

HOW TEMPLES WERE BUILT

If, after thousands of years, we can still identify the gods worshiped in the Egyptian temples and the kings who built them, and can still name the rooms and establish their cult functions in the over-all plan, it is thanks to their hieroglyphic inscriptions, reliefs, and decoration. These are essential elements of the architecture. They interpret the whole building, inside and out, as well as its portals, walls, columns, and ceilings; they also evoke with their own power the meaning and perpetuation of the daily ritual, and of the special ceremonies during the great festivals. Starting with the New Kingdom the reliefs on temple walls increasingly show the kingly role in the various phases of the liturgy. They ratify for eternity the sense of the ritual drama that symbolized the world order, and they elevate the mystery into a tangible, logical reality that is ever present. Not only the cult image in its sanctuary but the whole temple, with all its chapels, gates, pillars, reliefs, inscriptions, and emblems, was seen as having an existence which, after sleeping through the darkness of the night, had each morning to be ritually aroused from their slumber if the movement of the natural order was to continue.

Some idea of how a temple was built at Heliopolis by King Sesostris I may be gained from the text of a leather scroll. Under the aegis of the king the plans were discussed among his high officials and entrusted to the royal keeper of the seal, who directed the execution. With full pomp the king, accompanied by the high priests and the "scribe of the sacred book," betook himself to the building site to perform there the foundation-laying ceremonies.

The construction of a building with such awesome implications for the entire world order required special motives, thorough planning, and elaborate preliminary ceremonials before any real construction began. At Edfu this ceremony was based on a treatise by Imhotep, King Zoser's architect, that was written during the Third Dynasty but contained rites that were even older. The first record of the ceremony is from the Second Dynasty, in reliefs on the outer wall of a granite shrine from Hierakonpolis, and they are still found in temple reliefs of the Late Period. The king set out

in festive procession, accompanied by the cult image, to the temple site. Here a ritual drama took place, in which the gods' roles were presumably taken by priests and priestesses. During the nocturnal hours the king fixed the four corner points and the correct orientation of the sanctuary as directed by the god Thoth, with the help of the stars. Then, aided by the goddess Seshat, he marked off the temple precinct by "driving in the stakes" and "stretching the cords." There followed a groundbreaking ceremony in which the king dug foundation trenches, filled them with white sand, a symbol of purity, and made the cornerstone sacrifice which, with the offerings, was buried at the four corners of the future building. Finally, in accordance with an immemorial custom that obviously goes back to the beginnings of Egyptian brick architecture, bricks were molded of Nile mud mixed with frankincense and placed at the four corners of the foundations. In this way the foundation stone was laid.

The reasons for erecting a temple were of many kinds. They lie in the demands of theology and of the priesthood, but especially in the royal obligation to maintain, with the gods, the world order. The architect of the temple, therefore, was the Pharaoh. The royal jubilee was the principal occasion for building temples, large and small, to symbolize the eternal continuance of the dynastic succession and confirm the close relations between the king and the gods.

The planners of an Egyptian temple had to take into account the entire prevailing theological system, the nature of the principal god for whom the sanctuary was to be built and those of his co-deities, together with all their festivals and cult requirements. Accordingly the details of the plan had to be worked out by a large team of theologians, translated into drawings, and presented for the king's approval. The designs of the late temples of Edfu and Dendera went back to ancient temple plans and to the treatise written by Imhotep. There are sketch plans of smaller sanctuaries and of a royal tomb complex of the New Kingdom on papyrus and limestone tablets; the plan of the temple at Heliopolis is on the back of an inventory tablet. In translating from the sketched plans to the building site a square grid was probably used, though at Kalabsha it was composed of rectangles.

But who were the architects and what were their tasks? We have already mentioned Imhotep, the architect of King Zoser's mortuary precinct and the tomb complex of his successor. His titles and functions, preserved on a statue of his royal master, were "chief sculptor, high priest of Heliopolis, hereditary prince, the first after the king, and keeper of the seal of the king of Lower Egypt." In 470 B.C. the Persian king Darius dispatched Khenem-ib-Ra, a chief architect working under Amasis, the last great ruler of the Twenty-Sixth Dynasty, to lead an expedition to obtain stone blocks from the Wadi Hammamat. There he has left us his family tree, carved in the cliff. As proof of a long and prestigious professional tradition, he lists twenty-two generations of architects, starting with Kanofer, architect of King Khasekhemui (end of the Second Dynasty). The names of numerous architects have been handed down from all periods of Egyptian history; some tombs and statues bearing long biographical inscriptions have been preserved. The Egyptian language has no word for "architect"; each master-builder was called "director of all the king's works." They held a special position of trust in relation to the king and frequently acted as his vizier as well. In the New Kingdom, architects began their careers by entering the government service as "apprentice scribes." This reinforces the impression that their principal duties were organizational: recruiting and allocating labor, and procuring building materials, especially supervising the quarrying of stone and its transport from distant quarries to the capital. In inscriptions they boast of their outstanding technical achievements, such as the erecting of obelisks and colossal statues. Only rarely do they refer to the buildings they erected, and never to creative ideas.

ANCIENT NEAR EAST GENERAL WORKS

FRANKFORT H., *Art and Architecture of the Ancient Orient*, London, 1954.

LLOYD S., *Art of the Ancient Near East*, London, 1961.

PIGGOTT E.S., ed. *The Dawn of Civilization*, London, 1961.

PORTOGHESI P., ed. *Dizionario enciclopedico di architettura e urbanistica*, Rome, 1968-69.

PREHISTORY

GARSTANG J., *Prehistoric Mersin*, Oxford, 1953.

LLOYD S., and SAFAR F., "Tell Hassuna," in *Journal of Near Eastern Studies*, vol. IV, no. 4, 1945.

MELLAART J., *Catal Höyük: A Neolithic Town in Anatolia*, London, 1967.

MELLAART J., *Earliest Civilizations of the Near East*, London, 1965.

THESIGER W., *The Marsh Arabs*, London, 1964.

MESOPOTAMIA

General works:

BEEK M.A., *Atlas of Mesopotamia*, London, 1962.

STROMMENGER E., and HIRMER M., *5000 Years of the Art of Mesopotamia*, New York, 1964.

Sumerians and Akkadians:

DELOUGAZ P., *The Oval Temple at Khafaje*, Chicago, 1940.

DELOUGAZ P., and LLOYD S., *Pre-Sargonid Temples in the Diyala Region*, Chicago, 1942.

DELOUGAZ P., HILL H.D., and LLOYD S., *Private Houses and Graves in the Diyala Region*, Chicago, 1967.

FRANKFORT H., LLOYD S., and JACOBSEN T.H., *The Gimil-Sin Temple and the Palace of the Ruler at Tell Asmar*, Chicago, 1940.

LLOYD S., and SAFAR F., "Tell 'U-'qair," in *Journal of Near Eastern Studies*, vol. II, no. 2, 1943.

PARROT A., *Sumer*, London, 1960.

WOOLLEY C.L., *The Development of Sumerian Art*, London, 1935.

WOOLLEY C.L., *Ur Excavations*, vol. V: *The Ziggurat and Its Surroundings*, London, 1939.

Second millennium:

ANDRAE W., *Das Wiedererstandene Assur*, Leipzig, 1938.

BAQIR T., "Dur Kurigalzu," in *Iraq*, supplement 1944-45, and *Iraq*, vol. VIII, 1946.

PARROT A., *Mission Archéologique de Mari*, vol. II: *Le Palais*, Paris, 1958.

Assyrian and Neo-Babylonian period:

JACOBSEN T., and LLOYD S., *Sennacherib's Aqueduct at Jerwan*, Chicago, 1935.

LOUD G., *Khorsabad*, vol. II, Chicago, 1938.

MACQUEEN J.G., *Babylon*, London, 1964.

MALLOWAN M.E.L., *Nimrud and Its Remains*, London, 1966.

PARROT A., *Nineveh and Babylon*, London, 1961.

PARROT A., *Assur*, Paris, 1961.

IRAN AND THE LEVANT

GODARD A., *The Art of Iran*, London, 1962.

HARDEN D., *The Phoenicians*, London, 1962.

POPE A. UPHAM, *Survey of Persian Art*, London, New York, 1938.

SCHMIDT E., *Persepolis*, vol. I, Chicago, 1953.

YADIN Y., *The Art of Warfare in Biblical Lands*, London, 1963.

ANATOLIA

General works:

AKURGAL E., *The Art of the Hittites*, New York, 1962.

LLOYD S., *Early Highland Peoples of Anatolia*, London, 1967.

NAUMANN R., *Architectur Kleinasiens*, Tübingen, 1955.

Bronze and Iron Ages:

AKURGAL E., *Phrygische Kunst*, Ankara, 1955.

BLEGEN C.W., *Troy and the Trojans*, London, 1963.

LLOYD S., and MELLAART J., *Beycesultan*, 3 vols., London, 1962-72.

ÖZGUC T., *Altintepe*, Ankara, 1966.

PIETROVSKI B.B., *The Kingdom of Van and Its Art*, London, 1967.

PIGGOT E.S., *Vanished Civilizations*, London, 1963.

This bibliography is limited to modern works containing plans, reconstructions, and photographs, with brief descriptions and comments. The primary sources can be found in numerous archaeological reports listed in the bibliographical appendices of the general works indicated above.

EGYPT

Landscape and monuments of Egypt and Nubia:

BAEDEKER K., *Ägypten und der Sudan, Handbuch für Reisende*, Leipzig, 1928.

Egypte, Encyclopédie de voyage, Geneva, Paris, Munich, 1969.

KEES H., *Das Alte Ägypten, eine kleine Landeskunde*, Berlin, 1955.

PORTER B., and MOSS, R.L.B., *Topographical Bibliography of Ancient Egyptian Hieroglyphic Texts, Reliefs, and Paintings*, vols. I-VII, Oxford, 1927-51.

SCHLOTT A., *Die Ausmasse Ägyptens nach altägyptischen Texten*, Darmstadt, 1969.

History of ancient Egypt:

DERCHAIN P., "Le Rôle du roi d'Egypte dans le maintien de l'ordre cosmique," in *Le Pouvoir et le Sacré: Annales du Centre d'Etudes des Religions*, I, Brussels, 1962, pp. 61-73.

FRANKFORT H., *Kingship and the Gods: A Study of Ancient Near-ern Religion as the Integration of Society and Nature*, Chicago, 1958.

JACOBSOHN J. H., "Die dogmatische Stellung des Königs in der Theologie der Alten Ägypter," in *Ägyptologischen Forschungen*, vol. 8, Glückstadt, 1939.

MORET A., *Du caractère religieux de la royauté pharaonique*, Paris, 1902.

POSENER G., *De la divinité des pharaons*, Paris, 1960.

WILDUNG D., "Die Rolle ägyptischer Könige im Bewusstsein ihrer Nachwelt, I," in *Münchner Ägyptologische Studien*, 17, Berlin, 1969.

Egyptian culture of the archaic period:

BADAWY A., "La Première architecture en Egypte," in *Annales du Service des Antiquités d'Egypte*, no. 51, Cairo, 1951, pp. 1-28.

COTTEVIEILLE-GIRAUDET R., "Rapport sur les fouilles de Médamond (1931): Les Monuments du Moyen Empire," in *Bulletin de l'Institut Français d'Archéologie Orientale*, IX, Cairo, 1933.

JÉQUIER G., "Les Temples primitifs et la persistance des types archaïques dans l'architecture religieuse," in *Bulletin de l'Institut Français d'Archéologie Orientale*, VI, Cairo, 1908, pp. 25-41.

REYMOND E.A.E., *The Mythical Origin of the Egyptian Temple*, Manchester, 1969.

History of Egyptian art in general:

DONADONI S., *Arte egizia,* Turin 1955.

HAMANN R., *Ägyptische Kunst, Wesen und Geschichte.* Berlin, 1944.

LANGE K., and HIRMER M., *Ägypten. Architektur, Plastik, und Malerei in drei Jahrtausenden,* Introduction by E. Otto and C. Desroches-Noblecourt, Munich, 1957.

MÜLLER H.W., *Ägyptishe Kunst: Monumente alter Kulturen,* Frankfurt, 1970.

SMITH W.S., *The Art and Architecture of Ancient Egypt,* Baltimore, 1958.

STEINDORFF G., *Die Kunst der Ägypter,* Leipzig, 1928.

WOLF W., *Die Kunst Ägyptens, Gestalt und Geschichte,* Stuttgart, 1957.

WOLF W., *Il mondo degli Egizi,* Rome, 1958.

YOYOTTE J., "Egypte ancienne," in *Encyclopedie de la Pléiade.*

Egyptian architecture:

BADAWY A., *A History of Egyptian Architecture,* vols. I-III, Cairo, 1954; Berkeley and Los Angeles, 1966 and 1968.

BADAWY A., *Architecture in Ancient Egypt and the Near East,* London, 1966.

BORCHARDT L., "Zur Geschichte des Luqsortempels," in *Zeitschrift für ägyptische Sprache und Altertumskunde,* XXXIV, Berlin - Leipzig, 1896.

BORCHART L., "Agyptische Tempel mit Umgang," with drawings by Herbert Ricke, in *Beiträge zur Ägyptischen Bauforschung und Altertumskunde,* vol. 2, Cairo, 1938.

CAPART J., *L'Art égyptien,* vol. I: *L'Architecture,* Brussels, Paris , 1922.

DAVIES N. DE GARIS, *The Mastaba of Ptahhetep and Akkethetep at Saqqarah* (Archaeological Survey of Egypt, 8/9), 2 vols., London, 1900-1901.

DE CENIVAL J.L., *Egypte, Epoque pharaonique,* Freiburg, 1964.

DE CENIVAL J.L., *Ägypten, Das Zeitalter der Pharaonen,* Munich, 1966.

GIEDION S., *The Beginnings of Architecture,* New York, 1963.

HAENY G., "Basikale Anlagen," in *Beiträge zur Ägyptischen Bauforschung and Altertumskunde,* vol. 9, Wiesbaden, 1970.

HÖLSCHER U., "Medinet Habu. Ausgrabungen des Oriental Institutes des Universität Chicago, Ein Vorbericht," in *Morgenland: Darstellung aus Geschichte und Kultur des Ostens,* 2, Leipzig, 1933.

JÉQUIER G., *L'Architecture et la décoration dans l'ancienne Egypte,* vols. I-III, Paris, 1920-24.

LAUER J.P., *La Pyramide à degrés: L'Architecture,* 3 vols., Cairo, 1936-39.

OTTO E., and HIRMER M., *Ancient Egyptian Art: the Cults of Osiris and Amon,* New York, 1967.

PETRIE W.M.F., "The Royal Tombs of the First Dynasty," with a chapter by F.L. Griffith, in *Eighteenth Memoir of the Egypt Exploration Fund,* part I, London, 1901.

PORTOGHESI P., ed., *Dizionario enciclopedico di architettura e urbanistica,* Rome, 1968-69.

SMITH E.B., *Egyptian Architecture as Cultural Expression,* New York, London, 1938.

VANDIER J., *Manuel d'Archéologie Egyptienne,* vol. II, 1 and 2: *L'Architecture funéraire, religieuse et civile,* Paris, 1954-55.

LIST OF PHOTOGRAPHIC CREDITS

NOTE: *Photographs by Bruno Balestrini.*
All those supplied by other sources are gratefully acknowledged below.
The numbers listed refer to the plates.

Bildarchiv Foto Marburg, Marburg/Lahn: 111, 140, 144, 156, 157, 168, 188, 189, 208, 227, 232, 235

Borromeo, F., Milan: II, III, XIII, XVI, XVIII, XIX, XX, XXI, XXII, XXIII, XXIV

British Museum, London: 13, 75, 76, 83, 84, 86, 87, 88, 89, 95, 96, 100, 101, 102, 103

Ciriani, N. / Stradelle, Milan: IX, X

Director General of Antiquities, Iraq Museum, Baghdad: 22, 25, 26, 27, 28, 41

Hirmer Verlag, Munich: 35, 36, 179, 230, 231, 233, 248

Institut français d'archéologie, Istanbul: 92

Müller, Prof. H.W. Irschenausen:

139, 145, 175, 194, 209, 228, 234, 246, 247, 249

Oriental Institute, University of Chicago: 38, 73, 81, 107

Pellegrini, L., Milan: I, IV, VI, VII, VIII, XI, XII, XIV, XV, XVII, XXV

Perissinotto A., Padua: 57, 58, 59, 61, 125, 126, 128, 130, 131, 133, 135, 137

Powell J., Rome: 90, 92

Saint Hugh's College, Oxford: 6

Service des Documentations Photographiques des Musées Nationaux, Paris: 40, 74, 82, 136

Sinclair J.A., Ltd., London: 12

Staatliche Museen, Berlin: 16, 43, 118, 122, V

Warburg Institute, London: 47